D0486372

RECIPES FOR AN ARABIAN NIGHT

Recipes for an Arabian Night

TRADITIONAL COOKING FROM NORTH AFRICA AND THE MIDDLE EAST

David Scott

PANTHEON BOOKS, NEW YORK

Illustrations Copyright 1983 by Hutchinson
Publishing Group
All rights reserved under International and Pan-American
Copyright Conventions. Published in the United States by
Pantheon Books, a division of Random House, Inc., New
York, and simultaneously in Canada by Random House of
Canada Limited, Toronto.
Originally published in Great Britain as *Traditional Arabic
Cookery* by Hutchinson Publishing Group.

Library of Congress Cataloging in Publications Data

Scott, David, 1944–
Recipes for an Arabian night.

1. Cookery, North Africa.   2. Cookery, Near Eastern.
I. Title.
TX725.N67S36   1984   641.5961   83-43162
ISBN 0-394-72292-2 (pbk.)

BOOK DESIGN BY GINA DAVIS

Manufactured in the United States of America

First American Edition

CONTENTS

Acknowledgments vi

Introduction vii

Customs ix

Cook's Notes xi

Glossary xiv

Basic Ingredients and Methods xix

MEZZE (HORS D'OEUVRE) 3

SOUPS 33

BREADS, PIES, AND SAVORY PASTRIES 49

SALADS 65

FISH 79

MEAT AND POULTRY DISHES 95

GRAINS, BEANS, AND LENTILS *(Including Kibbi and Couscous)* 127

STUFFED VEGETABLES *(Mishshi)* 151

DESSERTS AND SWEET PASTRIES 163

DRINKS 181

Index 187

I would like to thank Eve Bletcher, my most favorite cook, for testing some of the recipes.
Steve Hardstaff for his illustrations and the enjoyment of watching his ideas come to life on paper.
Jean Kilshaw, whose expert and accurate typing turns a messy manuscript into pleasing order.

INTRODUCTION

The origins of Arabic cooking can still be seen today in the cooking of the Bedouin tribes that crisscross the deserts of North Africa and Arabia. The food is simple and reflects the needs and possibilities of nomads in a land of scant vegetation. Grilled or boiled lamb, unyeasted whole-wheat bread baked on a hot griddle, mixed meat and vegetable dishes called *tagine*, yogurt, and, for special occasions, rice covered in seasoned, melted butter are typical foods. Other early influences on Arabic cooking were provided by the peasant dishes of the countries surrounding the deserts, particularly the cooking of Egypt, which also influenced early Jewish cooking. Later, after the death of Muhammed in A.D. 632 and the subsequent invasion of many countries by Muslim Arabs, more overriding influences were brought to bear. The warrior Muslim Arabs moved out of the deserts and invaded vast territories including, initially, Lebanon, Jordan, Iraq, and Syria, the hub of the present-day Middle East and later Persia, which at this time, perhaps, wrought the greatest influence on the cooking of the Muslim empire. To the west they invaded North Africa, Spain, and Portugal.

These diverse influences produced a many-faceted and rich cuisine of beautiful and elaborate dishes. However, throughout the Middle East the original simple Bedouin influence has persisted, and this book will concern itself with Arabic cooking in which economy and simplicity enhanced by the imaginative use of seasoning, color and presentation are the main features. This, the author believes, reflects cultural changes in the Arab world where more and more people, both men and women, are involved in the hurly-burly of city life, so that simple food, prepared with the same love and care but in a shorter time, is more suitable than the elaborate and time-consuming feasts of old. These are still enjoyed but only on special occasions.

In the recipes given in this book the basic ingredients—lamb, poultry, whole-wheat bread, rice, yogurt, and eggplant—are combined and complemented with other grains, beans, vegetables, white fish, and meats to produce a variety of flavorsome, healthful, and economical dishes. The traditional Arabic sweet tooth is represented in the chapter on desserts.

Because of the diverse influences on Arabic cooking and the regional as well as national differences in the names and methods of preparation of often basically the same dishes, I have not tried to categorize or delineate a particular style. I have chosen dishes that the Western cook is likely to want to prepare and can prepare simply, and which also represent the cooking of the Arabian deserts and the lands that surround them. I make no claims that the book is in any way comprehensive. The recipes I have included come from the Fertile Crescent—Lebanon, Syria, Jordan, and Iraq; from North Africa—Morocco, Tunisia, Egypt, and Algeria; and from the Gulf States—Yemen, Saudi Arabia, Kuwait, Bahrein, Oman, and Muscat. The name of the region or—if the source is clear—the individual country of origin is usually given. If no source is named, it means that the dish is available in most Arab countries.

There has been some unavoidable overlap with my book *Middle Eastern Vegetarian Cookery,* and some basic or common recipes appear in both books. However, I have kept this to a minimum and where appropriate offered suitable variations.

CUSTOMS

The origins of the Arab people are closely linked with the nomadic tribes, later to be called Bedouin, who inhabited the Arabian peninsula more than five thousand years ago. These people developed a sophisticated ethical and behavior code that was in sharp contrast to the simple trappings of their lives. Their desert environment was dangerous, and survival often depended on mutual support. Hospitality to visitors, friends or strangers, became a serious obligation, a duty as well as a pleasure, and this same attitude to guests still holds fast in Arab society. Food and drink are automatically offered to guests, and they should not be refused. The host is careful not to ask questions or discuss topics such as politics or religion that might provoke disagreement with his guests, and in this way he can behave in the most generous manner and allow his guests to feel at home without putting into question his own integrity on matters that concern him. Strangers are given the same welcome, and according to Bedouin tradition, even enemies are entitled to two full days' refuge and then safe conduct to the nearest boundary. Hence there is considerable ritual involved in host-guest relations, and much of this revolves around the serving and partaking of food.

The food and drink are served either on a cloth spread over a carpet or on a large brass or copper tray resting on four low wooden legs. Guests sit on low cushions around the food with the most important guest sitting nearest to the host. All the various dishes are presented simultaneously and the diners eat them in their own order of preference. Traditionally the food will be eaten with fingers or with pieces of flat bread used as scoops. Only the right hand is used, and this will be washed at the table. The thumb and first two fingers are used, but if the food is soft it is permissible to use five. Using the thumb and first finger is considered a sign of pride. Nowadays, however, it is more common to be provided with plates and cutlery, although it is still likely that the host will select particularly tasty pieces of food to offer his most favored guest.

Talk and music are not encouraged while eating, and it is only after the meal, when coffee is being served, that discussion and merriment are free to take place. Because most Arab countries are Muslim, no alcohol will be available, but there will be a narghile (hookah) pipe to share. Customarily women and men do not eat together, and what is more, the men take their pick of the food first! I'm not sure the first tradition would bother all women, but I'm sure the second would, so here is one idea where at your own table you might override Arab custom.

Muhammed = messenger (from God)
Islam = submission (to God)
Muslim = those who submit (to God)
Koran = recitation or discourse

COOK'S NOTES

Arabic cooking techniques are economical and uncomplicated because they evolved from a nomadic way of life in which simplicity was most important. The average family kitchen in the West will have all the equipment that is normally needed. I recommend a blender or food processor for making dips and a mortar and pestle for crushing spices.

The Arabic cook uses, where possible, natural unrefined ingredients, and dishes prepared from a selection of meat, fish, poultry, grains, legumes, vegetables, fruits, nuts, yogurt, cheese, herbs, and spices provide a naturally balanced diet. Good diet is a long-standing Arab tradition, and as early as the tenth century Arab philosophers were extolling the virtues of healthful eating. Most of the ingredients needed are readily available, and unusual ones can be obtained from the specialist food shops that are now open in most towns.

A generous use of herbs and spices is common in Arabic recipes, and in the Middle East they are all available fresh in the spice streets of the town bazaars. In the West we may sometimes have to make do with dried herbs or ready-ground spices. The most commonly used herbs and spices are parsley, mint, oregano, fennel, cumin, coriander, cayenne, cardamom, cloves, nutmeg, saffron, turmeric, ginger, paprika, black pepper, and sesame seeds. Tahini, a paste made from crushed sesame seeds, is frequently used in the preparation of bread dips and sauces.

In the desert, cooking oil is traditionally prepared by rendering sheep's tails, and is called *alya*. In the towns olive oil, other vegetable oils, and *samneh*, a type of clarified butter, are most common. If you can afford it, use olive oil; otherwise, a good unsaturated seed oil such as sesame or sunflower is an excellent substitute. Where a vegetable oil is stipulated in a recipe, one of these oils is recommended.

The most popular vegetables are eggplants. They are used in the preparation of everything from hors d'oeuvre to salads to main meals. Onions, tomatoes, red and green peppers, zucchini, garlic, cucumber, lettuce, radishes, and olives are also common, and any vegetable that can be stuffed to make *mishshi* will also be eagerly bought. Lemons too are used much in cooking.

Nearly all meat dishes are made from lamb or mutton. Sheep travel well and can live on poor pasture, hence their popularity. Until recently beef was rare, and pork is forbidden by Muslim dietary laws. Nowadays, with the advent of deep freezing and an increase in popularity, beef is becoming more common, but by meat, an Arab still means lamb or mutton. Meat is considered a luxury, and Arab dishes that contain meat will probably need only a half, or less, of the amount used in a similar Western recipe. Feast days are an exception, and on those days a whole lamb or sheep may be killed and eaten.

Chickens are bred in all towns and villages, and poultry is popular. Fish, except in coastal areas and those near to inland seas, is generally expensive and a rare treat.

Wheat is the chief grain, followed by rice. Basmati-type rice is the most favored. Lentils, chick-peas, and ful medames are popular legumes, although a huge variety of beans is sold.

Yogurt, usually homemade, is used for dips, soups, salad dressings, sauces, and marinades. Blended with a little water and salt and chilled, it makes a refreshing and nourishing drink called *aryaan*.

Pastries, cakes, and biscuits, which are much liked, are made usually with pastry, honey, chopped nuts, dried fruit, and rose water. They are normally eaten between meals, and fruit ices, sorbet, or fresh fruit is eaten as dessert. After the meal or at any time during the day very sweet strong black coffee or tea is served.

Thus in summary the following most common ingredients would provide the basis for preparing all the recipes in this book.

HERBS (*fresh or dried*)	MEAT AND POULTRY	VEGETABLES
coriander leaves	*beef (occasionally)*	*cucumbers*
fennel	*chicken*	*eggplant*
mint	*lamb or mutton*	*garlic*
oregano		*lettuce*
parsley	OILS	*onions*
	clarified butter	*red and green peppers*
SPICES	*olive oil*	*tomatoes*
black pepper	*unsaturated vegetable oil*	*zucchini*
cardamom		
cayenne	GRAINS, BEANS, NUTS	OTHER INGREDIENTS
cloves	*almonds*	*fila pastry*
coriander	*burghul wheat*	*honey*
cumin	*chick-peas*	*lemons*
ginger	*ful medames*	*olives*
nutmeg	*lentils*	*rose or orange blossom*
paprika	*pine nuts*	*water*
saffron	*rice (preferably Basmati*	*tahini*
sesame seeds	*type)*	*vine leaves*
turmeric	*walnuts*	*yogurt*
	whole-wheat flour	

In Basic Ingredients and Methods, I have given a description of some of the techniques that are made use of more than once in the book. A recipe for yogurt, which accompanies most Arabic meals, is included. A recipe for pita bread, which partners yogurt at the table, is given in the chapter on Breads, Pies, and Savory Pastries.

GLOSSARY

This contains words that may not appear in the text but which I thought would be useful to the traveler in the Middle East who is interested in food. Where a choice of names is given the first one is the Arabic name. This is not necessarily the name used in the text, where for unusual ingredients or dishes I have used the name by which they are best known.

In the text I have generally given a recipe its Arabic name if this reflects a particular area of origin. For common dishes made in a variety of countries, each giving it their own name, I have given the recipe only its English title.

The Arabic spellings I have chosen for the Glossary are those most used in Arab countries. However, Arabic peoples differ as to the correct way to spell Arabic words in English. Consequently, you may find the same item spelled in a variety of ways in recipes from different countries.

AISH	see Pita bread.
ALYA	rendered fat from sheep's or lamb's tail used for cooking.
ARAK	an anise-flavored alcoholic drink made from grape or date spirit.
ARYAAN	a popular drink made with water, salt, and yogurt.
BAHARAT	a spice mixture used in Iraq and the Gulf States consisting of pepper, coriander, cinnamon, cloves, nutmeg, and paprika.
BAKDOUNIS	Arabic name for parsley, much used as a cooking herb and for garnishing. The Arab cook prefers the flat-leafed, stronger-flavored varieties.
BAKLAWA	Arabic name for the sweet pastry better known in the West as baklava, in which layers of paper-thin pastry sheets are buttered and stuffed with a nut filling and baked.
BAMIA	Arabic name for okra, a popular vegetable in the Middle East. Known as ladies' fingers in India.

BURGHUL	also known as bulgur, bulgar, and cracked wheat, it is a wheat product made by parboiling whole wheat grains, drying them in the sun, and then crushing them in a stone mill. Used in the preparation of *kibbi*.
COUSCOUS	the national dish of Morocco, Tunisia, and Algeria, in which grains of couscous, a semolina product, are steamed over a spiced casserole of meats and vegetables.
FALAFEL	deep-fried chick-pea croquettes, similar to the Egyptian *ta'amia* (which use dried white broad beans).
FILA, FILO, or PHYLLO	a paper-thin dough used to make sweet and savory pastries.
FUL, FOOL, or FOUL	general name for beans, as well as referring more specifically to fava or broad beans.
FUL MEDAMES	brown beans used to make the Egyptian dish of the same name.
FUL NABED	large broad beans used to make *ta' amia*, which are deep-fried bean croquettes, a very popular snack food in Egypt.
HAB-HAL	cardamom, a spice used in sweet and savory dishes and particularly for flavoring Arabic coffee. Pods, seeds, and ground cardamom are available.
HALOUMY	salty milk cheese (goat, sheep, or cow) made in Lebanon.
HARIRA	a thick soup, traditionally served to break the fast during Ramadan.
HARISSA	a hot spicy North African sauce used to flavor couscous. It is made from cayenne, cumin, garlic, salt, and olive oil.
HILBEH	fenugreek.
HUMMUS	chick-peas.
HUMMUS BI TAHINI	a bread dip made from ground chick-peas, garlic, and tahina.
JORN	mortar of pestle and mortar.

KAMMOUN	cumin, crushed cumin seeds have a delicious aromatic aroma very good for flavoring all sorts of dishes. In Arabic cooking it is usually used in conjunction with coriander and perhaps garlic.
KHOBZ	unyeasted Arab bread.
KIBBI or KIBBEH	a mixture of pounded meat and burghul (cracked wheat), eaten raw, baked, or fried. The national dish of Syria and Lebanon.
KISHK	a product made from fermenting together milk, burghul, and yogurt, then drying and grinding the mixture to a powder. It keeps well and provides a source of nourishment as a drink.
KONAFA or KADAYIF	a popular sweet pastry made from a shredded pastry filled with nuts and soaked in syrup.
KOUBIZ-ARABI	Arabic name for pita bread.
KOUZBARA	coriander, an herb and a spice. The chopped leaves are used in salads and as a garnish in the same way as parsley. The seeds, which have a mild, sweetish flavor, whole or crushed, are widely used in the preparation of a variety of dishes.
LABAN	yogurt.
LABNA	yogurt cheese.
LOOMI	dried lime peel, used whole or powdered.
MADAQUI	pestle of pestle and mortar.
MAHLAB	a Syrian spice prepared from the stone of the black cherry.
MANSAF	a formal bedouin banquet of whole roast lamb and rice.
MASGEOF	to grill or broil. More specifically it describes a way of grilling fish over wood, popular in Iraq.
MAWARD	rose water, a fragrant liquid distilled from rose petals and used in both savory and sweet dishes for its flavor and aroma. Sold in a concentrated form or diluted ready for use.
MAZAHER	orange blossom water, a scented liquid distilled from orange blossoms. It is used to flavor sweet pastries and puddings.

MELOKHIA, MILOUKIA, MILOOKHIYYA	the young shoots of a green, jutelike plant used for their thickening properties and color in soups, particularly in Egypt. The flavor resembles that of spinach. Also, the soup made with it.
MEZZE or MEZE	Middle Eastern hors d'oeuvre; often a wide variety will be served as a substitute for a main meal.
MISHSHI	stuffed vegetables.
PITA, PITTA, AISH, KHOBZ, KHOUBIZ, KESRA, KMAJ	Arabic bread. A soft-textured, flat, slightly leavened bread with a hollow in the middle, made in a variety of shapes and sizes.
RAKI	Turkish anise-flavored alcoholic drink similar to *arak*.
SAMNEH or SAMNA	clarified butter, also known as *ghee*.
SBAR	tamarind, a bitter-flavored spice. It has to be soaked before use.
SESAME SEEDS	oily, nut-flavored, nutritious seed used fresh or toasted, particularly in bread and cake making. Tahini is made by crushing the seeds into an oily paste.
SFIHA or SFEEHA	small spicy lamb pies.
SHRAK	whole-wheat bread baked over a hot dome.
SMEED	semolina, flour produced from the inner, branless center of durum wheat grain. Used to make couscous grains.
SNOBAR	pine nuts or pignoli, small, white or cream-colored nuts used fresh or roasted. They are obtained from the cones of particular types of pine tree and impart a distinctive, delicious flavor to sweet or savory dishes, especially pastries or rice dishes.
SORJ	a metal dome heated over a fire over which bread dough is draped and baked. See *Shrak*.
TABBOULEH	Lebanese or Syrian salad made from burghul wheat, lots of parsley, and lemon juice.
TAGINE	North African stew.

TAHINI or TAHINA	a paste made from sesame seeds, used to make salad dressings, bread dips, and sauces. It has a creamy nut taste.
TA' AMIA	see *Ful nabed*.
TARATOOR	a sauce made from tahini, lemon, and garlic.
TUM	garlic.
WARAK-DA-WALI	leaves of the grapevine, best known as one of the wrappings used for dolmas (stuffed vegetables).
ZA'ATAR	an herb similar to marjoram and oregano.
ZAFFARAN	saffron, the stigma of crocuses. Sold in dried strands or powdered. Used for coloring and flavor, particularly in rice dishes. Turmeric is a cheap substitute.
ZATAR	an Arabic term for thyme. It also describes a mixture of herbs that includes thyme, used to flavor breads.
ZHUG	Yemenite hot spice mixture of caraway seeds, cardamom, garlic, hot peppers, and coriander crushed together.

BASIC INGREDIENTS
AND METHODS

Yogurt (Laban)

Yogurt with its health-giving qualities accompanies most Arab meals, and it also provides a refreshing drink when diluted with water, salted, and slightly chilled. Each household will probably have its own particular method of preparation handed down from mother to daughter. Arabic yogurt tends to be more tart than its Western counterpart and more refreshing. The preparation is not complicated and, once you have developed the right routine, almost foolproof. Start with a batch of live yogurt from a health-food store or just plain commercial yogurt and then use your own yogurt to start the next lot. Your first attempt may produce a quite thin yogurt, but this is not unusual, and by the third or fourth batch, when the culture has improved, you will be making thick creamy yogurt.

> *2 or 4 cups milk*
> *1 or 2 tablespoons plain yogurt*

Bring the milk to a boil in a clean pan. To be sure of obtaining a thick yogurt stir 1–2 tablespoons of powdered milk into the fresh milk before starting. Remove the milk from the heat and pour it into a bowl. Leave to cool until you can just comfortably dip your fingers in it and leave them there for 10 seconds, without hurriedly pulling them out. Stir in the live yogurt, cover the bowl with some kind of lid or plate, and wrap it in a thick towel. Store it in a warm place, approximately 70° F, and leave it to set for 10–12 hours. Transfer the bowl to the refrigerator and chill. The longer you leave the yogurt fermenting in a warm place the more tart it becomes. Finally it goes sour and is not very tasty.

Yogurt cannot be used in cooking without first being stabilized as described on page 156. It can, however, be made into a sauce which is then poured hot (but not boiled) over a cooked dish. See recipe below for a sauce that can be served with vegetables, meat, or rice dishes.

YOGURT SAUCE WITH MINT
FERTILE CRESCENT

Makes 3½ cups

This sauce can be stored in the refrigerator for as much as 3 days. It should be reheated in a double boiler.

4 tablespoons butter
2 cloves garlic, put through a garlic press
1 teaspoon salt
2 tablespoons finely chopped fresh mint or 2 teaspoons crushed dried mint

2 cups yogurt
1 egg, beaten
½ cup water

Melt the butter in a small pan and add the garlic, salt, and mint. Lightly sauté and set them aside. Beat the yogurt, egg, and water together and transfer them to a small heavy pan. Cook, while stirring, over moderate heat without allowing the mixture to boil. Stir in the garlic mixture and continue cooking and stirring, without boiling, for a further 5 minutes. Remove from the heat and the sauce is ready for use.

YOGURT CHEESE
(Labna)
LEBANON

Makes 2½ cups

This delicious soft cheese is simple to make from homemade yogurt. It is excellent spread on pita bread, sprinkled with a little olive oil, and served with salad and olives. This is a traditional Lebanese breakfast.

2 cups yogurt
salt

Put the yogurt, salted to taste, into the center of a doubled piece of cheesecloth, draw up the corners, and tie them securely. Hang the ball of yogurt over a bowl to drain and leave for 10–12 hours, or overnight. Alternatively, line a colander with cheesecloth, pour in the yogurt, salted to taste, and leave over a plate for 10–12 hours, or overnight to drain off. Remove the cheese from the cheesecloth and transfer it to the refrigerator in a covered container. The longer you leave the yogurt draining—up to 36 hours outside the refrigerator, or up to 3 days inside—the firmer the cheese will become.

VARIATION: Combine the prepared cheese with 1–2 cloves of crushed garlic, a little chopped fresh mint, parsley or basil, black pepper to taste, and 1–2 teaspoons of olive oil. Mix well together and serve on bread.

Clarified Butter (Samneh)

Clarified butter or *samneh* (ghee in Indian cooking) is, next to olive oil, the favored cooking fat of the Arabic cook. It keeps for months without refrigeration and does not burn as easily as butter when cooking. In all the recipes where butter is stipulated as the cooking medium, *samneh* may be substituted.

Melt the butter in a pan over a low heat and then bring to a low bubbling boil. Froth will rise, which is then skimmed off. This contains the unwanted milk solids and any salt present. Pour the remaining melted butter through a doubled piece of cheesecloth into a glass jar and store for use as required.

Fila Pastry (Ajeen)

Fila is a delicate paper-thin pastry very popular throughout the Middle East and used to make a variety of savory and sweet pastries. The Arabic name is *ajeen*, which is also the collective name for "pastry." Since fila is possibly the name by which this product is best known in the West, I have used it here. Fila pastry is very versatile: the sheets are flexible and can be rolled or folded in a variety of ways, either singly or in stacks. Making fila at home requires a lot of skill, patience, and time, and nowadays it is normally bought ready prepared. It is quite easily obtained here from Greek food stores. For those of you who are interested in trying your hand at making the pastry, here is a good recipe.

4½ cups plain white flour
¾ teaspoon salt
3 tablespoons olive oil

Sift the flour and salt into a mixing bowl and stir in 1 cup of water and the oil. Kneed the dough by hand for about 10 minutes. (Alternatively, use a food processor for the mixing and kneading.) The dough should become smooth and elastic. Cover it with a clean cloth and leave it to rest at room temperature for 1 hour.

Divide the dough into 10 equal portions and shape each into a square. Take one square at a time and roll the pastry on a floured surface into an 8-by-5-inch rectangle. Dust the pastry and work surface with flour and roll the pastry sheet onto the middle of a wooden dowel about 2 feet long and ½ inch in diameter. Press and roll the pastry back and forth with both hands to form a sheet of about 10 by 16 inches. Unroll the pastry, dust it and the work surface again with flour, and roll the pastry back onto the dowel, this time from the opposite end. Repeat the rolling procedure to form a finished sheet of fila pastry of 12 by 20 inches. Place it on a piece of wax paper, and cover it with another piece of wax paper. Repeat the rolling procedure for each square of dough, laying each finished pastry sheet on top of the wax paper that covers the previous sheet.

This recipe makes about 10 sheets of fila pastry. They are thicker than the shop-bought variety; 1 sheet of homemade pastry is equal in thickness to about 2 sheets of shop-bought. Otherwise use the pastry as directed below for commercially produced fila pastry.

Commercially produced fila pastry keeps for weeks under refrigeration. It is normally sold in standard size packs of 1 pound or 8 ounces containing twenty-four or twelve sheets respectively. The normal size of a leaf of pastry is 20 by 12 inches. Once a pack has been opened or the pastry is exposed to the heat of the kitchen, the sheets start to dry out and become crumbly. Thus remove from the wrap only as many sheets as you intend to use immediately, and brush them with melted butter to retain their flexibility. Alternatively, store the unwrapped sheets between two dry tea towels and drape over the top a third tea towel that has been dampened. Remove the sheets of pastry only as required. Do not worry if sheets tear while you are using them; if a sheet is badly torn, leave it in position and cover it with another buttered sheet. Since the sheets are so thin, adding one more does not affect the basic preparation of a pastry dish.

Nuts

Nuts are much used by the Arab cook for making savory and sweet stuffings, in rice dishes, sauces, bread dips, cakes, sweet dishes, and many others. Pine nuts, almonds, pistachios, walnuts, and hazelnuts are some of the varieties available. Pine nuts in particular are delicious cooked with other foods, and they are most popular with Arab cooks. The nuts grow inside the hard outer casing of the familiar pine cone and have no shell except for a thin casing. They are white or cream-colored with a soft texture. Their flavor is best brought out by roasting. There are many different types of pine trees with edible seeds in North America, but they have never really been exploited except by Native Americans.

To Blanch Nuts   Pour boiling water over the kernels in their skins. Leave to soak for 3–4 minutes, drain, and squeeze or rub the nuts out of their skins, using thumb and forefinger.

Chopping, Slicing, and Grinding Nuts   For coarsely chopped nuts place them in a food processor and switch the machine on for just a few seconds. Leave it longer to grind or mill the nuts completely. Lacking a grinder, put the nuts in a wooden bowl and chop them with a sharp vegetable knife. For fine grinding use a pestle and mortar. To slice nuts use a sharp knife and slice each nut individually. If the nuts are very hard try boiling them first.

Roasting Whole or Chopped Nuts   Preheat the oven to 350° F. Spread the nuts on a baking tray and place it in the oven. Bake for about 5 minutes, giving them a shake once or twice during cooking. The nuts are ready when lightly browned. They may also be pan-roasted on top of the stove. Put the nuts in an ungreased or, if you wish, a lightly oiled heavy frying pan and lightly toss them over a moderate flame.

Buying and Cooking Beans

Buy your beans or lentils from a reputable and busy health food store or a good produce market, since, although beans can be stored for a long time, they can get tough if kept too long. Store them in airtight containers in a dry, coolish place. Nearly all beans need soaking before cooking to ensure they are digestible. Between 12 and 14 hours is usually long enough. Measure the beans you require, pick over them to remove any grit or stones, and cover them in cold water. Leave for the soaking period, drain them, put them in the pan, add 5 cups of water per 1 cup of beans, bring to the boil, reduce the heat, cover, and simmer until tender. Some beans tend to foam when first cooked; remove the foam by skimming with a slotted spoon.

To Prepare Eggplants for Cooking

Slice or cube the eggplants into the shape required. Sprinkle liberally with salt and set the eggplant pieces in a colander with an inverted plate on top of them. Leave them for an hour or two to allow the bitter juices to soak away. Rinse the eggplants well to remove all the salt. Pat dry on a clean cloth. The eggplants are now ready for frying, sautéing, casseroling, and so on.

General Salad Dressing

Increase the amounts proportionately to suit the quantity you require.

4 tablespoons olive oil or other vegetable
  oil
3 tablespoons lemon juice
salt and black pepper to taste

VARIATIONS: Add 1 or more cloves of garlic, put through a garlic press.
  Add 1 or more tablespoons of chopped fresh parsley, mint, or other herbs.

Stock

For a number of the recipes a stock can be used in place of the water specified. Substituting stock for water will normally add to the flavor of the dish. The following ingredients are suitable for making stocks: the water in which beans, unsalted meat, fish, or poultry have been cooked; bones of all types, cooked and uncooked; cooked and uncooked trimmings of meat, fish, or poultry; giblets; chopped root vegetables; other vegetable trimmings such as carrots, onions, tomatoes, celery, potatoes, and greens (cabbage, lettuce, root tops).

To make the stock, crack any large bones, then put them with all the other ingredients used into a pot. Cover with water, bring to the boil, and skim off any scum that rises to the surface. Reduce the heat, season to taste with salt and black pepper, cover, and simmer for 1 hour.

Vine Leaves

Vine leaves are picked from the grapevine early in the summer when they have darkened in color but are not yet the dark green of mature leaves. The leaves are shiny on one side and dull on the other. They are sold fresh in the countries of origin, where they are used in the preparation of dolmas (vine leaves stuffed with a rice filling) and fresh in salads. For export the leaves are slightly blanched in boiling salted water and then packed in brine in cans or sealed plastic packets. For details on how to prepare fresh, canned, or packaged vine leaves for stuffing, see the recipe for stuffed vine leaves on page 23.

Chopping and Grinding

The traditional methods of fine chopping with a knife and grinding with a pestle and mortar can be replaced advantageously in terms of time and efficiency by a food processor. Herbs, vegetables, nuts, cheese, beans (particularly for bread dips), and meat may all be chopped or ground in the processor. If you have one, you should use it where appropriate in preparing the recipes in this book.

Burghul Wheat

Burghul wheat, also known as bulgar and cracked wheat, is a wheat product that has been made since ancient times in parts of Western Asia, Eastern Europe, and North Africa. It has excellent nutritional qualities and a fine taste, and lends itself to many ways of cooking.

Burghul is prepared by parboiling whole wheat grains in a minimum amount of water. The wheat is then spread thinly on a cloth or tray, dried out (traditionally in the sun), and finally cracked between stone rollers. The starch in the grain is gelatinized by the boiling water, and after drying and cracking this results in a hard, vitreous product. The boiling also diffuses part of the wheat germ and bran into the starchy center of the grain, and if the wheat is then cracked or milled, the product retains all the goodness of the whole grain.

Burghul wheat is cooked by steaming or boiling, sometimes after being roasted first (see pages 136–37 for cooking methods). It can be bought in various grades ranging from fine to coarsely ground. Sometimes the makers parboil and roast the burghul before packaging to make it a fast-cooking product.

Burghul flour can be substituted for some of the regular flour in bread making. Dough made with burghul flour needs more kneading than ordinary wheat dough, but it does bake into beautiful bread. Because of the nutritious wheat germ, burghul flour does not keep well except under refrigeration. Buy enough flour for your immediate needs only, or best of all, if you have a hand mill at home, grind your own as needed.

Burghul has a special place in the cooking of the Middle East, and is the basis of kibbi, the great traditional dish of Syria and Lebanon. It also has a long culinary tradition in Jewish cooking and is even mentioned in the Bible, where it is described as a food particularly attractive to young men (see Zechariah 9:17).

Tahini

Tahini is made from lightly roasted sesame seeds. It is very simple to make with a food processor.

To make 2 cups of tahini, you will need 4 cups of white sesame seeds, hulled. Preheat the oven to 325°F. Spread the seeds evenly over the bottom of a shallow baking tray and put the tray on the middle shelf of the oven. Roast the seeds, shaking them occasionally, for 7 or 8 minutes. They should not brown. Leave the seeds to cool and then place them in a food processor. Using a metal blade, grind the seeds until they form a smooth paste (about 5 minutes). Pour and scrape the tahini into a clean screwtop jar. Use as required. It will keep for several months.

Harissa

Harissa is a hot pepper sauce of North African origin. It is traditionally used to accompany couscous.

2 tablespoons crushed dried chili peppers or cayenne	2 teaspoons caraway seeds
2 teaspoons ground cumin	2 cloves garlic
	1 teaspoon salt

Combine the ingredients and grind them together in a pestle and mortar, blender, or food processor. Store the harissa in a clean dry jar. Use directly from the jar when adding to the couscous stew. To make harissa sauce for serving in a small dish as an accompaniment to the finished couscous, cook the harissa with 2–3 tablespoons of olive oil over a low heat for 5 minutes.

RECIPES FOR AN ARABIAN NIGHT

Mezze

(HORS D'OEUVRE)

Simple Mezze
Roasted Chick-Peas
Stuffed Dates
Cucumber with Feta Cheese
Cucumber with Yogurt
Shrimp Pâté
Smoked Herring and Garlic
Anchovy or Sardine Fingers
Spicy Fried Fish
Grilled Cheese
Fried Cheese
Chick-Peas and Mixed Nuts
Tahini and Cumin Dip
Zahtar
Spiced Eggplant Dip
Taratour Bi Tahini
Baba Ghanooj
Hummus Bi Tahini
Ful Medames
Ful Nabed

Falafel
Falafel Hot Sauce
Falafel Relish
Green Beans in Oil
Artichoke Hearts in Oil
Dolmas (Stuffed Vine Leaves,
    Stuffed Cabbage Leaves,
    Stuffed Swiss Chard)
Lamb Patties
Lamb and Burghul Wheat
    Cakes
Chicken Meatballs
Lamb Kebabs
Shish (Ground Meat) Kebabs
Lamb Brain Salad with
    Dressing
Fried Lamb Brains
Lamb Tongues with Tahini
Tabbouleh (Burghul Wheat
    Salad)
Arabian Omelet

ezze or appetizers are part of the way of life of the Arabic world. They are served at the beginning of a meal or as a meal in itself, as snacks or accompaniments to drinks at any time of the day or night. The more auspicious the occasion the wider the variety of mezze offered. They are prepared in numerous ways, and the selection offered is limited only by the cook's repertoire and the ingredients available.

Probably the best known mezze in the West are the two bread dips, *hummus bi tahini* and *baba ghanooj* and the Egyptian bean dish of *ful medames*. These mezze lend themselves very well to the Arabic way of eating in which the diner uses a piece of flat bread to neatly scoop food from the central serving dishes. Recipes for these and other dips and other interesting mezze including dolmas, tabbouleh, falafel, lamb patties, chicken meatballs, kebabs, and lamb's tongue are given in this chapter.

A further variety of mezze can be prepared by making half quantities of the various rice dishes, meat dishes, salads, stuffed vegetables, and savory pies and pastries given in the book. Equally, many of the mezze, made in a large enough quantity, are excellent as main dishes or light meals.

All the mezze dishes can be prepared 3-4 hours in advance and stored in the refrigerator until ready to serve, unless the recipe states otherwise.

SIMPLE MEZZE

Olives on their own or in salad dressing or spiced with a little cayenne
Nuts, a single variety or mixed, plain or lightly roasted
Slices of onion and tomato arranged in a circle of alternating rings, garnished
with chopped parsley or mint
Wedges of cucumber
Yogurt, slightly salted
Chick-peas, soaked, drained, roasted in the oven, and salted
Pickles

Green beans, cooked, dressed in oil and lemon juice
Artichoke hearts or okra in olive oil
Slices of salted or smoked fish
Cottage cheese or yogurt or both, mixed with tahini and sprinkled with cumin seeds
Shredded, chopped, or sliced raw vegetables
Slices of hard-boiled egg, dusted with cinnamon, coriander, and salt
Lemon wedges
Radishes on ice
Fried shrimps or mussels
Fresh dates stuffed with soft cheese
Fresh dates in yogurt
Tahini seasoned with crushed garlic and lemon juice to taste
Ripe avocado flesh mixed with finely chopped onion and tomato, seasoned with salt and black pepper, dressed with lemon juice, and served on lettuce leaves

ROASTED CHICK-PEAS
LEBANON

Makes about 1½ pounds (2½–3 cups)

2 tablespoons olive oil
2 cloves garlic, put through a garlic press

3¾ cups cooked or canned chick-peas, drained weight
Salt

Heat the oven to 400° F. In a heavy frying pan heat 1 tablespoon of oil. Add 1 clove of garlic and cook for 1 minute over a low heat. Add half the chick-peas and cook, stirring, for 5 minutes. Transfer the contents of the pan to a bowl. Repeat the procedure, for the remaining oil, garlic, and chick-peas. Spread the chick-pea mixture out on a baking sheet and place it in the oven for 5–10 minutes. Turn the mixture about twice during this time. Put the chick-peas into a warmed serving bowl and serve at once.

STUFFED DATES
(Tamar Al Gibna)
GULF STATES

Serves 4

> 24 fresh dates
> 4 ounces cream cheese or ricotta cheese
> 24 roasted almonds

Carefully cut open the dates just enough to remove the pits. Stuff each cavity with cream or ricotta cheese and top with a roasted almond. Serve with any leftover cheese in a separate bowl.

CUCUMBER WITH FETA CHEESE
(Michoteta)
EGYPT

Serves 4

> 1 medium cucumber, peeled and diced
>   (seeding optional)
> 1 medium onion, finely diced
> 6 ounces feta cheese
>
> 2 tablespoons olive oil
> juice of 1 lemon
> salt and black pepper

Combine the cucumber and onion and mix well. Crumble the feta cheese into a separate bowl. Beat in the oil, lemon juice, and salt and black pepper to taste. Pour the mixture over the cucumber and onion and serve with pita bread.

CUCUMBER WITH YOGURT
LEBANON

Serves 6

1 medium cucumber, peeled and diced
  (seeding optional)
2 cups yogurt
2 or more cloves garlic, put through a
  garlic press

salt and pepper to taste
2 tablespoons finely chopped fresh mint
  or 2 teaspoons crushed dried mint
a few sprigs fresh mint or crushed dried
  mint for garnish

Put the cucumber in a serving bowl. Beat the yogurt and garlic together and season to taste with salt and black pepper. Stir in the mint. Pour the mixture over the cucumber. Garnish with sprigs of fresh mint (or sprinkle with crushed dried mint) and serve with pita bread.

SHRIMP PÂTÉ
EGYPT

Serves 4 to 6

This pâté, which requires no cooking (except for the shrimp), is available along Egypt's Red Sea coast.

12 ounces fresh shrimp or 8 ounces
  canned shrimp
½ cup coarse bread crumbs
2 tablespoons butter
6 black or green olives, pitted and
  chopped
½ cup nuts (almond, pine, or walnuts),
  lightly roasted

juice of 1 lemon
2 tablespoons finely chopped parsley
2 cloves garlic, put through a garlic
  press
½ teaspoon finely chopped or grated
  fresh ginger (or use ground ginger)
½ teaspoon cumin
salt and black pepper to taste

For garnish:
reserved shrimp
lemon slices
olives

If you are using fresh shrimp, shell and devein them and fry them in a little olive oil until tender. Now combine all the ingredients (reserve a few whole shrimp) in a blender or food processor and purée the mixture to a smooth consistency. Transfer it to a 2-pint pâté tureen, lightly oiled, or form it on a plate into a square pâté shape. Garnish the top with a pleasing pattern of whole cooked shrimp, lemon slices, and halved olives. Chill for 3–4 hours before serving. To remove from the tureen, run a knife around the edge of the pâté, then slip a spatula underneath it and gently prise it out.

SMOKED HERRING AND GARLIC
FERTILE CRESCENT

Serves 4

2 small smoked filleted herrings, cut
   into small pieces
2 cloves garlic, finely diced
juice of 1 lemon

4 tablespoons olive oil
2 tablespoons finely chopped parsley
pita bread

Combine the first 4 ingredients, sprinkle with parsley, and serve with pita bread.

ANCHOVY OR SARDINE FINGERS
NORTH AFRICA

Serves 4 to 6

This North African dish is quick to prepare and tasty. Serve it as part of a selection of mezze.

1 tablespoon finely chopped fresh mint
   or parsley
½ teaspoon grated nutmeg
1 small can anchovies or sardines in oil

fingers of toasted bread
freshly ground black pepper to taste
black olives, halved

Combine the mint or parsley and the nutmeg. Drain the oil from the fish and then roll them individually in the parsley or mint and nutmeg mixture. Place them on the fingers of toast, sprinkle with pepper, and finally garnish with olives.

SPICY FRIED FISH
JORDAN

Serves 4

For this Jordanian dish mackerel has been given in the recipe, but you can also use 1½ pounds of fillets or steaks of cod, haddock, halibut, or sole, or the same amount of whole herring, mullet, or bass, cleaned and filleted.

2 medium-size (¾ pound) mackerel, cleaned and filleted	½ teaspoon cumin
2 tablespoons olive oil, or sesame seed or sunflower seed oil	¼ teaspoon cayenne
1 medium onion, sliced	juice of 1 lemon
2 cloves garlic, put through a garlic press	2 tablespoons water
	salt and black pepper to taste

Cut each fish into 4 slices and fry them in the oil in a heavy frying pan until light golden on both sides. Push them to one side in the pan. Add the onion and garlic, and fry them until soft. Redistribute the fish around the pan and add the remaining ingredients. Cover and simmer over a low heat for 15 minutes. Adjust the seasoning. Arrange the fish slices on the serving dish and pour the sauce from the pan over them. Chill and serve.

GRILLED CHEESE
EGYPT

Serves 4

The best cheese for this mezze is a hard goat cheese. Haloumy cheese (sometimes available in Greek delicatessen shops) is traditionally used. It also works with a hard Cheddar that has dried out. You can leave a piece of Cheddar out to dry or use those pieces of cheese not put away from the dinner party the night before.

8 ounces hard, dry cheese, cut into ¾-
  inch cubes

Cover the broiling pan with aluminum foil and lightly oil the foil. Place the cubes on top and broil them until the top side starts to blister. Turn and repeat for three sides of the cube. Alternatively, if the cheese will hold together, skewer the cubes and grill them like kebabs.

Both grilled cheese and fried cheese (see recipe below) should be prepared and cooked just before serving.

FRIED CHEESE
EGYPT

Serves 4

Use the same type of cheese as above. Serve with bread and wedges of lemon.

olive oil or sesame seed oil
8 ounces hard, dry cheese, sliced into
  2-inch squares ½ inch thick

juice of 1 lemon
bread
1 lemon, cut into wedges

Heat a serving dish in the oven. Add enough oil to a small, heavy frying pan to cover the bottom with a thick film. Gently heat the oil and then add the cheese cubes. Heat through, turning once or twice. Squeeze on the lemon juice, being careful of spitting oil. Transfer all the contents of the pan to the hot serving dish and serve immediately.

CHICK-PEAS AND MIXED NUTS
FERTILE CRESCENT

Serves 6

1¼ cups chick-peas, soaked overnight,
  drained
about 2 cups mixed nuts or seeds (e.g.
  almonds, hazelnuts, walnuts, pine
  nuts, pumpkin seeds)

juice of 2 lemons
salt

Preheat oven to 450° F. Place chick-peas and mixed nuts in a pan and add the lemon juice and just enough water to cover. Bring to the boil, reduce heat, add salt to taste, and simmer for 10 minutes. Drain, discard the liquid, and spread the chick-pea/nut mixture on a flat baking tray. Place in the oven and roast until the nuts are just browned all over. Shake the tray once or twice during the roasting. Salt to taste. Serve immediately or store in an airtight container until required—not more than a day later.

BREAD DIPS

TAHINI AND CUMIN DIP

Makes 1¾ cups

1 cup tahini (see page xxvi)	up to ½ cup water
2 cloves garlic, put through a garlic press	½ teaspoon ground cumin
	½ teaspoon cumin seeds
juice of 1 lemon	1 tablespoon finely chopped parsley

Put the tahini in a bowl and whisk it until it is smooth and homogeneous. Stir in the garlic and lemon juice and mix well. Add water slowly, while whisking, until the dip is a consistency to your liking. Stir in the ground cumin and serve the dip garnished with cumin seeds and parsley.

ZAHTAR
FERTILE CRESCENT

Serves 6

This is a mixture of crushed seeds and nuts into which pieces of bread are dipped after first dipping them in olive oil. *Zahtar* can be made the day before serving and stored in an airtight container.

½ cup walnuts or hazelnuts	¼ cup cumin seeds
½ cup coriander seeds	salt and black pepper
1 cup sesame seeds	

Put all the ingredients except the salt and pepper in a blender or food processor, or use a pestle and mortar, and gently blend or crush the mixture to a dry crumble. Be careful not to form the mixture into a paste. Season to taste with salt and pepper. Put the *zahtar* on a plate and serve with olive oil and bread.

VARIATION: If you can find cooked, salted, and dried chick-peas (sometimes sold in packets as a snack food) add ½ cup to the *zahtar* ingredients before crushing.

SPICED EGGPLANT DIP
SYRIA

Serves 4

2 medium eggplants or 1 large, washed, dried	2 or more cloves garlic
2 tablespoons olive oil	salt
	cayenne or chili sauce

Preheat the oven to 350° F. Rub the eggplants with a little oil and place them on a tray in the oven on a middle shelf. Bake them for 45 minutes or until the interiors are soft and well done. Peel the skin off them as soon as they are cool enough to touch. Put the flesh in a bowl or a food processor, add the garlic and oil, and beat them into a purée. Add salt and cayenne or chili sauce to taste. Chill and serve.

TARATOUR BI TAHINI
(Tahini Dip or Sauce)
FERTILE CRESCENT

Makes 1¾ cups

1 cup tahini	salt, black pepper and cayenne to taste
juice of 2 medium lemons	2 tablespoons finely chopped parsley
2–3 cloves garlic	

Beat or blend together the tahini, lemon juice and garlic (or use a food processor). Now add water very slowly to make either a thick or a thin mixture. Dips need to be thicker than dressings or sauces. Carefully season to taste with salt, black pepper, and cayenne, and if you wish for a tarter taste, add more lemon juice. Chill. If serving as a bread dip, liberally sprinkle with parsley, gently stirring in a little before serving.

BABA GHANOOJ
(Eggplant Purée)
FERTILE CRESCENT

There are a number of variations on this popular bread dip or accompaniment to meat or fish dishes. Some include tahini and others do not; an example of each is given below. The important part of the recipes, which is the preparation of the eggplants, is the same in each case.

WITHOUT TAHINI

Serves 4 to 6

3 tablespoons vegetable oil (olive oil is preferred)	juice of 1 lemon
2 medium or 1 large eggplant	2 tablespoons finely chopped parsley
2 cloves garlic, put through a garlic press	salt and black pepper to taste
	black or green olives

Preheat the oven to 350° F. Rub the eggplants with a little oil and place them on a tray in the middle of the oven for 45 minutes or until the interiors are soft and well done. Alternatively, and preferably, if you have the facilities and time, cook the eggplants on a grill over a glowing charcoal fire, turning them frequently until they are blistered and thoroughly cooked. Split the eggplants down the middle and scoop out the flesh. Combine the flesh with the garlic, lemon juice, oil, and half the parsley. Beat or blend, or use a food processor, until the mixture is a smooth paste. Season to taste with salt and pepper and, if it is too thick, add a little extra oil. Transfer it to a serving dish and garnish with the remaining parsley and the olives.

WITH TAHINI

Serves 6

2 medium or 1 large eggplant
2 cloves garlic, put through a garlic
  press
1 small onion, finely chopped
juice of 1 lemon
½ cup tahini

1 tablespoon vegetable oil (olive oil pre-
  ferred)
salt and cayenne pepper
2 tablespoons finely chopped parsley
tomato slices

Prepare the eggplants as described in the recipe above. Beat or blend together the eggplant flesh, garlic, onion, lemon juice, tahini, and oil (or use a food processor) until a quite smooth mixture is formed. Season to taste with salt and cayenne. Stir in half the parsley and transfer the mixture to a serving dish. Sprinkle it with the remaining parsley and garnish with tomato slices.

HUMMUS BI TAHINI
(Chick-pea and Tahini Dip)
FERTILE CRESCENT (SYRIA)

Serves 6

This is a good basic recipe and gives plenty of scope for you to adjust the taste of the hummus to your own taste. Serve the hummus with warm pita bread, olives, lemon wedges, and a fresh salad.

1¼ cups chick-peas, washed, drained,
  covered with water and soaked overnight or use 2 cups canned chick-
  peas and ignore the first paragraph
  of the recipe
4½ cups water

juice of 2 lemons
¾ cup tahini
3 cloves garlic, put through a garlic
  press
salt to taste

Garnish
olive oil
paprika

chopped parsley
reserved chick-peas

Drain the soaked chick-peas and place them in a heavy pot with the fresh water. Bring them to the boil and remove any foam that forms. Gently boil the peas for 1½ hours or until they easily crush between thumb and forefinger. Drain the peas and reserve any cooking liquid. Put aside 1 tablespoon of peas for later use as a garnish. The hummus can now be prepared, either using an electric blender or food processor, or by hand with a Mouli or a pestle and mortar. Both methods are described below.

ELECTRIC BLENDER OR FOOD PROCESSOR METHOD

Put the cooked peas, lemon juice, tahini, and garlic into the blender or processor with enough cooking liquid (and plain water, if needed) to allow the mixture to purée satisfactorily. If you are using canned chick-peas, the juice in the can, unless it is a brine solution, may be substituted for cooking liquid. Add salt to taste and, if needed, more lemon juice or tahini to taste. Blend again, and it's ready to be served. (See below for serving instructions.)

HAND METHOD

Press the cooked peas through a sieve or the fine blade of a Mouli, or crush in a pestle and mortar. Crush the garlic with some salt and add to the chick-pea paste. Stir in the lemon juice, tahini, and enough cooking liquid (and plain water, if needed) to form a smooth, creamy paste. Add salt to taste and adjust the quantities of lemon juice and tahini as required by your taste.

Serving Pour the prepared hummus onto a serving dish, sprinkle with paprika and chopped parsley, and pour 1–2 tablespoons of olive oil over it. Finally garnish with the reserved cooked chick-peas.

FUL MEDAMES
EGYPT

Serves 6

This traditional Egyptian dish can be served as a main meal (for breakfast in Egypt) accompanied by hot pita bread and a tomato and onion salad. For a mezze make half the quantity given in the recipe and season and garnish it yourself with the ingredients given, rather than leaving it to the individual as recommended in the recipe. *Ful medames* are small dried brown broad beans. In other Arabic countries they use a type of white broad bean called *ful nabed* to make a similar dish, and a recipe for this is given below as well. If *ful medames* are not available, use brown beans or any other small dried beans.

1 pound dried ful beans, soaked over-night and drained	*1 small onion or a few scallions, finely chopped*
salt	*finely chopped parsley*
2 cloves garlic, put through a garlic press	*ground paprika and cumin*
	tahini (optional)
olive oil	*chopped hard-boiled eggs sprinkled with*
quartered lemons	*turmeric (optional)*

Put the beans in a heavy saucepan with enough water to cover them by 1–2 inches. Bring them to the boil, reduce the heat to simmer, and cover the pot. Cook for 2–3 hours or until the beans are very tender and crush easily. Make sure the beans stay moist during cooking, adding a little boiling water as needed. After cooking, season the beans to taste with salt and stir in the garlic. Arrange all the other ingredients in small bowls or plates on the table and serve the hot beans in individual bowls. Each person seasons and garnishes his or her own bowl of beans from the garnishes available.

FUL NABED
IRAQ

The amounts given in this recipe are sufficient to make enough *ful nabed* for 2–3 people or as one dish in a selection of mezze. This dish should be prepared and cooked just before serving. Serve with hot pita bread.

1 cup dried ful nabed or broad beans,   juice of 1 lemon
   soaked 24 hours, drained   3 tablespoons olive oil
¼ cup dried lentils (red or brown),   1 tablespoon finely chopped parsley
   washed   black or green olives
salt

If you have the patience, skin the beans (or buy the preskinned broad beans that are available) by squeezing them firmly until the skin slips off. This process can be assisted by slitting the skin with the point of a knife or your nail. Alternatively, you can leave the skins on and risk that occasionally the beans will be a little chewy. Put the beans and lentils in a heavy pot with enough water to cover them by 1–2 inches. Bring them to the boil, reduce the heat to simmer, and cover the pot. Cook the beans for 3–4 hours or until they are very tender and crush easily. Season them to taste with salt after 2 hours. Make sure the beans stay moist during cooking, adding a little boiling water as needed. Ideally at the end of cooking time there should be no liquid left. Now put the contents of the pot into a serving dish and put aside to cool. Mix together the lemon juice and oil and stir them into the beans, gently mashing them a little as you do. Garnish the dish with the parsley and olives.

FALAFEL AND TA'AMIA
EGYPT AND YEMEN

Ta'amia and falafel are spicy deep-fried bean croquettes. In Egypt ta'amia, made from dried white broad beans, are a national dish with a long history. The idea was imported to Israel, where they substituted chick-peas and called the croquettes falafel. The recipe given below is for falafel, since chick-peas are generally easier to obtain than Egyptian white beans, although these may be substituted in the recipe if you wish and you may even wish to try a mixture of both beans. Serve the falafel as an hors d'oeuvre with one of the tahini dips given earlier in the chapter, plus a green salad and pickles. Alternatively, make the falafel hot sauce or falafel relish (recipes given below) and serve with one of these. For a filling snack stuff the hot falafel into half a split pita bread, pour the hot sauce, relish, or other dressing over it, and top with a portion of salad.

FALAFEL

Makes about 15 falafel

The falafel mixture can be prepared several hours in advance, leaving out the raising agent. When ready to serve, mix in the raising agent, let the mixture stand for the required time, then form the falafel and deep fry them.

1¼ cups chick-peas, soaked overnight and drained	1 teaspoon ground cumin
	½ teaspoon turmeric
2 cloves garlic, put through a garlic press	¼ teaspoon cayenne
	½ teaspoon baking powder
2 medium onions, finely chopped	salt and black pepper to taste
1 teaspoon ground coriander	vegetable oil for deep frying

Cover the soaked and drained chick-peas in water and cook them until they are soft (about 1 hour; 2–3 hours for broad beans). Drain, and reserve the water for a soup, if you wish. Now mash the chick-peas to a paste, which can be done by hand using a meat grinder with a fine blade, with a pestle and mortar, or in an electric blender or food processor. Combine the paste with the remaining ingredients (except the deep-frying oil), mixing them together thoroughly. Pound, blend, or grind this mixture once again. Leave it to rest for 30 minutes and then form into 14–16 balls. If the balls are sticky, roll them in a little flour. Deep-fry them in hot oil 4–5 minutes, turning now and again until they are brown and crisp. Drain them on absorbent paper, and serve hot.

The rising agent used in this recipe (baking powder) can be replaced by the same amount of dried yeast. If yeast is used, prove it with a little sugar and warm water before adding it to the other ingredients, and leave the falafel mixture for 1 hour rather than 30 minutes before cooking.

VARIATION: Cooked, mashed, or finely diced vegetables (such as potatoes, carrots, parsnips, celery, green bell peppers, or fennel), chopped nuts, caraway seeds, or other ingredients may be added to the falafel ingredients before the final blending.

FALAFEL HOT SAUCE

Makes 2 cups

about 2 cups canned tomatoes
juice of 1 lemon
3 cloves garlic, put through a garlic
  press
1 tablespoon finely chopped parsley

1 teaspoon brown sugar
chili sauce to taste (½ teaspoon makes
  a mild sauce; 1 teaspoon, a hot one)
salt to taste

Put all the ingredients into a small, heavy pan, bring to the boil, and simmer uncovered until the tomatoes break up (about 30 minutes). Adjust the seasoning and allow to cool.

FALAFEL RELISH

2 ripe tomatoes, peeled
¼ medium cucumber, seeded and finely
  diced
1 green pepper, seeded, deribbed, and
  finely diced

2 tablespoons finely chopped parsley
salt and black pepper
chili sauce, chili powder, or finely
  chopped dried chilies to taste

Mash the tomatoes and combine with other ingredients. Mix thoroughly and chill.

COOKED VEGETABLES IN OIL
FERTILE CRESENT

Vegetables cooked in oil with lemon juice, tomato purée, and sliced onion, and served lukewarm or cold, are a popular mezze. Artichoke hearts and green beans are the two most commonly used vegetables, and recipes for them are given below. Olive oil is normally used in dishes that are to be served lukewarm or cold, and this is stipulated in the recipes. If you wish to serve them hot, substitute butter for the olive oil. In each case you may, if you are in a rush or cannot obtain the fresh variety, use canned or frozen vegetables.

GREEN BEANS IN OIL

Serves 6

1 *pound fresh* or *frozen green beans* (string beans)	2 *cloves garlic, put through a garlic press*
1 *medium onion, finely sliced*	½ *teaspoon sugar*
3 *tablespoons olive oil*	*salt and black pepper*
3 *large tomatoes*	*juice of 1 lemon*

Wash the beans well; top and tail, and if necessary string them. (If you are using frozen beans, defrost them.) Cut the beans in half or if they are very long cut them into 2-inch lengths. Sauté the onion in the oil in a heavy pan until it is just soft, then add the tomatoes and cook until they are soft. Add the beans and stir well. Add the garlic and sugar and season to taste with salt and black pepper. Just cover the contents of the pan with water, cover, and simmer for 20 or 30 minutes or until the beans are very tender. Leave them to cool in the pan. Just before serving, squeeze the lemon juice over the beans.

ARTICHOKE HEARTS IN OIL

Serves 4 to 6

4–6 *globe artichokes* or 1 *small can artichoke hearts*	4 *tablespoons olive oil*
2 *lemons*	*salt and black pepper to taste*
	1 *teaspoon sugar*

Wash the artichokes and cut off their stems very close to the base. Cut one lemon in half and squeeze the juice from half of it into a large bowl of water. Now, proceeding one artichoke at a time, cut off and discard 3–4 layers of the hard outer leaves and then trim the tops of all the remaining (tender) leaves down close to the heart. Scoop out and discard the choke. Rub the exposed surfaces of the hearts with the unused half lemon and place the artichoke in the bowl of lemon and water. Repeat for each artichoke.

Arrange the artichokes in a casserole and add the remaining juice from the half lemon and the juice from the unused lemon, the oil, 1 cup water, seasoning, and sugar. Cover the pan and simmer over a low heat for 50 minutes to an hour. Cool the artichokes in the pan and serve the hearts whole, or cut in half if they are large.

For canned artichoke hearts, drain them, put them in a casserole, add the juice of 2 lemons, the oil, *no* water, seasoning to taste, and the sugar. Cover and simmer over a very low heat for 30 minutes.

DOLMAS

Dolmas is a general name for stuffed vegetables (*mishshi* in Arabic), although as far as mezze are concerned the name usually refers to stuffed vine or cabbage leaves and less often to Swiss chard. The stuffing is either rice and ground lamb or rice and vegetables. I have given recipes for two stuffings followed by instructions for preparing dolmas from the three leaves mentioned. If the dolmas are to be served hot, provide a bowl of plain yogurt with them. Otherwise drain off most of the liquid, core, and garnish them with slices of lemon and sprigs of mint or parsley.

RICE AND GROUND LAMB FILLING

Serves 6

1 medium onion, finely chopped
2 tablespoons olive oil or other vegetable oil
1½ tablespoons pine nuts (optional)
1 pound lamb, ground
1 cup cooked rice (long-grain or Basmati)

½ teaspoon allspice
2 cloves garlic, put through a garlic press
2 tablespoons finely chopped fresh parsley or mint
salt and black pepper to taste

Fry the onion in the oil until it is just soft. Add the pine nuts, if used, and gently fry for another minute or two. Combine with the remaining ingredients and mix thoroughly. Now follow the instructions given below for whichever dolmas you choose to prepare.

RICE AND VEGETABLE FILLING

Serves 6

2 cups cooked rice (long-grain or Basmati)
1 medium onion, finely diced
1½ tablespoons currants (optional)
2 tablespoons tomato purée
2 cloves garlic, put through a garlic
  press

2 tablespoons finely chopped mint or
  parsley
1 teaspoon ground cinnamon
salt and black pepper to taste

Combine all the ingredients, mix well, and follow the instructions given
below for whichever dolmas you choose to prepare.

STUFFED VINE LEAVES

Makes 30 to 40 stuffed leaves
Serves 4 to 6 as main course, 6 to 8 as mezze

1 cup canned or packaged vine leaves
  or 30–40 fresh leaves (see page xxiv)
filling mixture (see above)
juice of 2 lemons
1 tablespoon olive oil or other vegetable
  oil

water, vegetable or meat stock
lemon slices
sprigs of fresh mint or parsley

Put the canned, packaged, or fresh vine leaves in a large bowl and scald
them with boiling water. Leave them to soak for a few minutes to disen-
tangle themselves. Now drain them and rinse with cold water. Separate
the leaves as you stuff them or, better still, separate them first and leave
them to drain on absorbent paper, dull side up. Layer the bottom of a
heavy pan or casserole with any broken leaves, or about 10 full leaves in
all. With the remaining leaves take one leaf at a time, cut off the stem
if it has one, and place about 1 tablespoon of filling (see recipes above)
in the center. Fold the stem end of the leaf over the filling. Fold in the
sides and roll up carefully from the stem end, to form a nice firm packet
about 2 inches long. Layer the stuffed leaves into the pan, side by side
and seam side down. Sprinkle them with the lemon juice and olive oil

and add enough water or stock to just cover the dolmas. Place an inverted plate or saucer over the dolmas to hold them down. Cover the pot and simmer for 1 hour. Make sure the dolmas stay moist during cooking. Leave them to cool in the pot if you are serving them cold. Drain and arrange on a serving tray in neat straight lines. Garnish with slices of lemon and sprigs of mint or parsley.

STUFFED CABBAGE LEAVES

Makes 20 stuffed leaves
Serves 4 to 6 as main course, 8 as mezze

1 medium cabbage or 20 leaves	*water or vegetable or meat stock (see*
filling mixture (see above)	*page xxiv)*
juice of 2 lemons	*lemon slices*
1 tablespoon olive oil or other vegetable	*sprigs of fresh mint or parsley*
oil	

Wash the cabbage and trim the stalk. If you are able to do so easily, strip off the leaves from the cabbage intact and cut out any hard central stalks. Wash them again and dip them, a few at a time, into a pan of boiling salted water until they become wilted and pliable. If it proves difficult to remove the leaves from the cabbage without their splitting, put the whole cabbage into a pan of boiling salted water and leave for 3–4 minutes. Lift the cabbage out, drain it, peel off the leaves, and then proceed as above.

Line a large heavy pan or casserole with torn or additional leaves and any stalks or ribs that have been cut out. Now place a tablespoon of filling onto the edge of each cabbage leaf and roll it into a neat finger shape, folding in the sides as you go. Layer the stuffed leaves into the pan seam side down and angled so that they do not lie alongside each other. Sprinkle them with the lemon juice and oil and add enough water or stock to just cover the stuffed leaves. Cover the pan and cook gently for 1 hour. Make sure during cooking that the leaves always stay moist. Leave them to cool in the pot if you are serving them at room temperature. Drain and arrange them on a serving dish. Garnish with lemon slices and sprigs of mint or parsley.

VARIATION: If you plan to serve the dolmas hot, try adding 2 or 3 tablespoons of tomato purée to the water or stock before it is poured over the uncooked dolmas.

STUFFED SWISS CHARD

For six people you will need about 2 bunches of chard. Blanch the leaves very quickly in a pan of boiling water before stuffing them, and then proceed as for cabbage leaves.

LAMB PATTIES
FERTILE CRESCENT

Serves 4 as main course, 6 to 8 as mezze

These patties can be served on their own or covered in tomato sauce (see page 156) or with the tahini sauce given with this recipe. They can be prepared several hours ahead, but should not be broiled or fried until just before serving.

TAHINI SAUCE

¼ cup tahini
½ cup water
2 tablespoons lemon juice

1 clove garlic, put through a garlic press
salt and black pepper to taste

Combine all the ingredients and blend thoroughly. Put the mixture in a pan over a low heat and bring to a slow boil while you prepare the patties.

PATTIES

1 pound lean lamb, ground twice
1 small onion, finely diced
2 tablespoons finely chopped parsley
salt and black pepper
flour for dusting

3 tablespoons butter or olive or sesame seed oil
chopped almonds or pine nuts, lightly fried brown in a little oil

Combine the lamb, onion, parsley, salt, and pepper and work into a smooth mixture. Alternatively blend to a paste in a blender or a food processor, using the steel blade. Form the mixture into 8 patties. Dust each with flour and fry in the butter or oil in a frying pan until nicely browned on both sides. Put the patties on a warm plate. Pour the sauce into the frying pan, return it to the boil, then pour it over the patties. Garnish with chopped almonds or pine nuts.

LAMB AND BURGHUL WHEAT CAKES
FERTILE CRESCENT

Makes 8 to 10 cakes
Serves 4 as main course, 6 as mezze

These are good with a sharp yogurt dressing and green salad. They can be prepared several hours in advance, but should not be broiled or fried until just before serving.

1 pound burghul wheat, fine grade	*1 egg, beaten*
8 ounce lamb, ground twice	*1 teaspoon ground cumin*
1 medium onion, finely diced	*salt and black pepper to taste*
2 tablespoons flour	*oil for frying*

Cover the burghul wheat with water and leave to soak for 30 minutes. Drain it and press out any excess water. In a large bowl combine the burghul with all the other ingredients and thoroughly knead them into a homogeneous mixture. Form the mixture into 8 or more patties or cakes. Fry the wheat cakes in ¼–½ inch of oil until they are nicely browned on both sides.

CHICKEN MEATBALLS
IRAQ

Serves 4 as a main course, 4 to 6 as mezze

This recipe is very good for using up leftover cooked chicken. The same recipe can also be used with other types of ground meat. The meatballs can be served as a main dish with a yogurt or tomato sauce. They can be prepared several hours ahead, but should be broiled or fried just before serving.

1 thick slice of white or whole wheat
  bread
1 pound cooked chicken, ground
1 egg, beaten
½ teaspoon cumin powder

¼ teaspoon cayenne (optional)
  pinch of saffron or turmeric
salt and black pepper to taste
2 tablespoons finely chopped parsley
oil for frying
lemon wedges

Cut the crusts off the bread and dip the bread into a bowl of water. Remove it and squeeze out as much water as possible. Put the bread, chicken, egg, spices, salt, pepper, and parsley into a bowl and knead them into a homogeneous mixture. Form the mixture into walnut-size balls and fry them nicely brown in shallow oil. Serve with lemon wedges and sprinkle with lemon juice before eating.

LAMB KEBABS

Serves 4 as main course, 8 as mezze

To serve as a mezze for four, halve the given quantities of ingredients. Otherwise, with the amounts given, this dish can be served as a main course. Lean chicken may be substituted for the lamb. Salad, pita bread, and hummus or another bread dip are good accompaniments for kebabs used as a main course.

vegetable oil (sesame seed oil is recommended)
½ teaspoon ground coriander
½ teaspoon caraway or dill seeds
1 pound lean lamb from shoulder or leg
  cut into ¾-inch cubes
salt and black pepper to taste

4 medium tomatoes, halved
4 bay leaves
4 small onions, halved
2 tablespoons chopped parsley
1 lemon, cut in wedges

Combine the oil, coriander, caraway or dill seeds, salt, and pepper in a marinading dish and mix well. Add the lamb cubes and leave to marinate for 1–2 hours. Now push the lamb cubes, tomatoes, bay leaves, and onions onto 4 skewers, forming a colorful pattern. Gently rub the residual marinading oil onto the lamb, onion, tomatoes, and bay leaves. Grill the kebabs under, and close to, a medium broiler, turning frequently. When they are browned, turn the broiler down to low and cook for another 10–15 minutes or until the lamb is tender. Pour more oil over the kebabs if they start to dry up. Turn them occasionally. These are delicious when cooked on a charcoal grill. Make sure they stay moist with fat during the cooking time. Serve them very hot, garnished with parsley and wedges of lemon.

Both lamb kebabs and shish kebabs (see recipe below) can be prepared several hours ahead, and then fried or broiled just before serving.

SHISH (GROUND MEAT) KEBABS

Serves 4 as main course, 8 as mezze

1 pound lamb or beef, finely ground
1 medium onion, finely chopped or grated
2 tablespoons finely chopped parsley
½ teaspoon ground cumin
½ teaspoon ground coriander

salt and black pepper to taste
4 medium tomatoes, quartered (optional)
2 medium green peppers, seeded and deribbed, cut in wedges (optional)

Combine the meat, onion, parsley, spices, and seasoning and mix together with your fingers into a smooth paste. Take your time over this and knead the paste until it is soft and smooth. Form the paste into small balls about 2 inches in diameter. Using flat-type skewers, carefully impale the meatballs on them. If you use the vegetables, alternate the meatballs with pieces of tomato and green pepper.

Cook the kebabs over charcoal if you have barbecue equipment. Hot glowing embers provide the best cooking medium. Otherwise use the oven broiler. Put it on high heat, oil the broiler pan well, and lay the kebabs on top. Cook them close to the heat source, with constant turning, until the meat is cooked and browned all over (about 8–10 minutes).

LAMB BRAINS AND TONGUES

In the Arab world those parts of a lamb or sheep which we in the West do not value are sometimes the delicacies. Lamb brains are an example. Below are two recipes, one for brain salad, the other for fried brain. Both dishes are served as mezze.

LAMB BRAIN SALAD WITH DRESSING

Serves 6

1 pound lamb brains
2 teaspoons salt
1 tablespoon + 1 teaspoon white vinegar
1 medium head Romaine lettuce
4 tablespoons olive oil
juice of 1 lemon
1 tablespoon chopped parsley

2 cloves garlic, put through a garlic press
½ teaspoon sugar
½ teaspoon cumin
salt and black pepper to taste
2-3 medium-sized tomatoes, quartered
olives

Wash the brains and then put them in a basin of cold water with 1 teaspoon of salt and 1 tablespoon of vinegar. Leave them for 30 minutes, drain, and then carefully remove the thin outer skin or membranes with the tips of your fingers. Cut out any veins that you can see. Sometimes it's difficult to separate the skin from the brain; in this case, leave it on. Wash them again under cold running water, put them in a pan, and just cover them with water. Add 1 teaspoon salt and 1 teaspoon vinegar. Bring them to a very gentle simmer and cook for 30 minutes. Remove the brains, drain them thoroughly, and leave to dry and cool. Slice them and arrange the slices in a serving dish over a bed of lettuce. Combine the oil, lemon juice, parsley, garlic, sugar, cumin, and seasoning and mix well. Pour the dressing over the brains. Garnish with tomatoes and olives.

FRIED LAMB BRAINS

Serves 6

1 pound lamb brains
salt
white vinegar
flour

salt and black pepper to taste
oil for frying
juice of 1 lemon
paprika

Prepare and cook the brains as for brain salad (preceding recipe). Cut the cooked brains into ¾-inch slices and dip them in flour seasoned with salt and pepper. Fry them in shallow oil in a heavy frying pan until golden brown. This should not take more than a few minutes. Serve on a hot dish with fresh lemon juice and paprika sprinkled over them.

LAMB TONGUES WITH TAHINI
LEBANON AND SYRIA

Serves 6

1 pound lamb tongues
1 small onion, quartered
1 clove garlic
1 bay leaf
salt

3 tablespoons olive oil
juice of 1 lemon
tahini sauce (see page 13; make ½ the
    amount of the recipe)
lemon wedges

Soak the tongues in running water for 1 hour and then scrub them with a kitchen brush. Put them in a pan with the onion, garlic, bay leaf, and 2 teaspoons salt. Cover them with water and bring to a gentle boil. Cover the pan and simmer the tongues for 1½ hours or until they are tender. Remove the tongues, cool them, and peel off the skin. Cut them into thin slices and arrange in a bowl. Mix the oil and lemon juice and pour it over. Chill. Before serving pour a generous amount of tahini sauce over the tongues and garnish them with lemon wedges.

OTHER MEZZE

TABBOULEH (BURGHUL WHEAT SALAD)
LEBANON AND SYRIA

Serves 6 to 8

Tabbouleh is a lovely salad made with burghul (cracked) wheat and lots of parsley, mint, and lemon. It is refreshing, tangy, and easy to make, an excellent summer mezze salad. Tabbouleh is claimed by both the Syrians and Lebanese, but there is no defined recipe and the way the salad is prepared is very much up to individual taste. The recipe I have given is more a guide than a strict set of instructions, and you should alter the amounts used and add to or subtract from the ingredients to suit your own taste. The main rule is to use lots of fresh parsley.

1 cup fine burghul wheat
½ cup finely chopped onion and/or scallions
2 cups chopped fresh parsley
4 tablespoons chopped fresh mint or 4 teaspoons crushed dried mint (the fresh parsley and mint can be chopped in a food processor)

3 medium tomatoes, finely chopped
½ cup lemon juice
½ cup olive oil
1 teaspoon allspice (optional)
salt and black pepper to taste
1 Romaine lettuce head, washed and separated into leaves
wedges of lemon

Cover the burghul wheat with plenty of cold water and leave for 1 hour. Drain in a colander and squeeze out any excess water by gently pressing the wheat with your hand. Now spread the wheat on a cheesecloth or paper towel and leave to dry further. Put the swollen wheat into a large bowl and gently stir in the onions, parsley, mint, tomatoes, lemon juice, oil, allspice, salt, and pepper. Cover the surface of a large serving dish with a few lettuce leaves, which are then used to scoop up the salad. Pile on the tabbouleh. Garnish with lemon wedges.

Alternatively line individual serving bowls with lettuce leaves and pile the tabbouleh on top. Put the remaining lettuce leaves in a central bowl and use these for scooping up the salad.

ARABIAN OMELET
(Eggah)
EGYPT AND GULF STATES

Serves 4 as main course, 6 to 8 as mezze

This dish, possibly of Egyptian origin, is a firm, thick, and well-filled omelet. It is served in wedges either hot or cold and is suitable as a mezze or a main dish. The filling can be either one or a mixture of vegetables, cooked meat, chicken, or fish. In the recipe I have not specified a particular filling, but I have suggested possibilities.

⅓ cup butter
1 medium onion, finely chopped
2 cloves garlic, put through a garlic press
eggplant, cubed, salted, washed, and drained
spinach, finely chopped
mushrooms, sliced
leeks, chopped
zucchini, chopped

ground beef or lamb, or finely chopped beef or lamb
finely chopped cooked chicken
finely chopped cooked fish (the chicken and fish can be chopped in a food processor)
6 eggs, beaten
1 teaspoon crushed dried mint
salt and black pepper to taste

Melt half the butter in a heavy frying pan and sauté the onion and garlic until they are just soft. Add the selected filling and continue cooking until it is just tender. Transfer this mixture to a bowl. Beat together the eggs, mint, salt, and pepper, and stir the mixture into the cooked filling. Clean out the frying pan and then melt in it the remaining butter. Pour the *eggah* mixture back into the pan and cook over a very low heat for 15–20 minutes or until the *eggah* is set. Brown the top by putting the pan under a preheated broiler. Serve hot or cold, cut into wedges.

Soups

Almond Soup
Broad Bean Soup
Tomato Soup
Lentil Soup
Lamb and Lentil Soup
Tomato and Lentil Soup
Spinach and Lentil Soup
Rice and Lentil Soup
Noodle and Lentil Soup
Egg and Lemon Soup
Harira with Lamb
   and Chicken

Chick-Pea Harira
Egyptian Green Herb Soup
   (Melokhia)
Kishk Soup
Meatball Soup (Kufta Soup)
Chicken Stock and Meatball
   Soup
Lamb Stock and Meatball
   Soup
Yemeni Lamb Soup
Arab Fish Soup

rabic soups are usually substantial dishes that can be served as main meals. They are made from vegetables, cereals, peas, beans, and meats and sometimes contain all four types of ingredients at once. There is no one way of making an Arabic soup, and even traditional soups such as *harira* or *melokhia* have many variations. The recipes I have given can be used as guidelines, and you can if you wish substitute your own selection of ingredients. Remember to soak beans overnight if you are using them and to use inexpensive cuts for the meat soups. Spices selected from black pepper, cumin, coriander, allspice, cinnamon, paprika, and cayenne may be added to the cook's own taste, and finely chopped parsley or mint, freshly squeezed lemon juice, or olive oil may be used to garnish the finished soup. The different ingredients in a soup are added in accordance with their different cooking times. Hence the normal order would be meat and pulses first, root vegetables such as onions and carrots second, rice or pasta third, and watery vegetables that cook quickly, such as spinach or zucchini, last.

ALMOND SOUP
(Shorabat Loz)
FERTILE CRESCENT

Serves 4

3 cups stock (*vegetable* or *chicken*) (see page xxiv)	1 cup ground almonds
2 tablespoons butter	1 cup light cream
1 small onion, finely diced	salt and black pepper
2 tablespoons white flour	10 whole almonds for garnish

Bring the stock to the boil. Meanwhile melt the butter in a heavy saucepan and sauté the onions until just softened. Stir in the flour and blend well. Slowly add the boiling stock, stirring the onion mixture all the time. Now add the ground almonds, stir well, reduce the heat, cover, and leave to simmer for 15–20 minutes. Remove from the heat, stir in the cream, season to taste with salt and pepper, and serve garnished with whole almonds.

BROAD BEAN SOUP
(Shorabat Ful Nabed)
EGYPT

Serves 6 to 8

This Egyptian soup uses the same type of broad white bean described in the preparation of *ful nabed* in the chapter on mezze. These beans are very good if you can obtain them, but they require a long soaking time. If this puts you off making soup, try using the same method but substitute fava or navy beans and soak them only overnight. Or for a very quick soup, use canned cooked chick-peas, which require no soaking.

> *1 pound ful nabed (dried skinless broad beans) covered in water and soaked for 36 hours*
> *2 tablespoons olive oil*
> *juice of 1 lemon*
>
> *ground cumin*
> *salt and black pepper*
> *finely chopped parsley*
> *lemon wedges*

Drain the beans and rinse well. Put them into a pot with 7 cups water and bring to the boil. Reduce the heat, cover, and simmer for 1–1½ hours or until very soft. Blend the beans and liquid or if you do not have a blender drain off the beans, reserving the liquid, and mash the beans or push them through a sieve. Return the blended mixture or puréed beans and liquid to the pot, add the oil and lemon juice, and season to taste with cumin, salt, and pepper. Return to the boil. Serve and allow the guests to garnish their own soup with parsley and more lemon juice.

TOMATO SOUP
(Shurabat al-Mawzat)
YEMEN

Serves 6

This is a good soup to make when tomatoes are plentiful and cheap.

1 pound lamb or beef soup bones, washed
1 cinnamon stick
½ cup rice, washed

1½ pounds ripe tomatoes
salt and black pepper to taste
yogurt (optional)

Put the soup bones, 5 cups water, and cinnamon stick into a pot and bring to the boil. Reduce the heat and simmer for 1 hour. Skim any scum that forms off the top of the soup. Add the rice and simmer for a further 20 minutes. Meanwhile drop the tomatoes for 1–2 minutes into a pan of boiling water and then remove their skins. Take the bones out of the soup and add the tomatoes, salt and pepper. Leave to simmer for 10 minutes. Then gently mash the tomatoes with the back of a wooden spoon, and simmer for another 10 minutes. Serve the soup with a bowl of yogurt which can be spooned in as required.

LENTIL SOUP
(Shourabat Adas)
MOROCCO

Serves 6

A delicious version of lentil soup. It's served topped with fried garlic and onion and fresh lemon juice.

2 cups lentils (red, brown, or green), washed
5 cups water or stock
1 medium onion, finely diced
1 medium carrot, sliced
1 teaspoon ground cumin
juice of 1 lemon

salt and black pepper
2 tablespoons olive oil
2 cloves garlic, put through a garlic press
1 large onion, thinly sliced
lemon wedges

Put lentils in a heavy pot with the water or stock, add the diced onion and carrot, and bring to the boil. Reduce the heat, cover, and simmer for 1 hour or until the lentils are very soft. Blend the mixture or push it through a sieve. Return it to the pot and add cumin, lemon juice, and salt and pepper to taste. Return to a gentle simmer for 15 minutes. Heat the oil in a frying pan and sauté the garlic for a minute or two. Add the onion and fry until it is golden brown. Serve the soup in bowls and top each one with a portion of the browned onions and garlic. Serve a side dish of lemon wedges for extra lemon juice if needed.

VARIATIONS: This soup can be cooked with lamb bones or shanks for a meaty taste. In the Middle East it is often served with more oil than used in the above recipe, so provide extra oil at the table. Melted butter is also used in place of olive oil.

For a thicker soup add ½ cup uncooked rice or broken pasta 20 minutes before the end of cooking time.

LAMB AND LENTIL SOUP

Follow the basic lentil soup recipe above but add 8 ounces of stewing lamb, cubed and lightly fried, on all sides, with the lentils at the beginning of the recipe. Do not blend or purée this soup.

TOMATO AND LENTIL SOUP

Follow the basic lentil soup recipe above and add 1 pound ripe peeled and chopped tomatoes (or use canned tomatoes) at the same time as the cumin, lemon juice, and seasoning.

SPINACH AND LENTIL SOUP
(Adas bis-sileq)
GULF STATES

Serves 6

2 cups brown lentils, washed
4 tablespoons olive oil or other vegetable oil
2 cloves garlic, crushed
1 pound fresh spinach, washed and chopped, or 8 ounces frozen spinach, defrosted

2 tablespoons finely chopped coriander leaves (optional)
juice of 2 lemons
½ teaspoon ground cumin
salt and black pepper
1 medium onion, finely chopped
lemon wedges

Put the lentils and 5 cups water in a heavy pot and bring to the boil, reduce the heat, cover, and simmer for 1 hour. Heat half the oil in a frying pan and sauté the garlic. Add the spinach and fry, while stirring, until the spinach is wilted. Transfer this mixture to the soup pot, add the coriander leaves, lemon juice, and cumin, and season to taste with salt and pepper. Cover and gently simmer for 20 minutes. Meanwhile fry the onion in the remaining oil until golden brown and add to the pot 5 minutes before the end of the cooking time. Serve hot, with lemon wedges for extra lemon juice as required.

RICE AND LENTIL SOUP
(Adas biz-ruz)
EGYPT

Serves 6

3 tablespoons olive oil or other vegetable
  oil
2 medium onions, finely chopped
3 cloves garlic, crushed
2 cups red lentils
5 cups water or stock
½ teaspoon paprika

½ teaspoon coriander
½ teaspoon cumin
pinch of nutmeg
juice of 1 lemon
salt and black pepper
½ cup rice, washed

Heat the oil in a heavy pan and add the onion and garlic. Fry, while stirring, until the onion is very lightly browned. Stir in the lentils and mix well. Add the water or stock, spices, and lemon juice, and season to taste with salt and pepper. Bring to the boil, reduce the heat, cover, and simmer for 45–50 mintues, or until the lentils are starting to disintegrate. Add the rice and return to the boil, reduce the heat, cover, and simmer for 15–20 minutes or until the rice is very tender. Adjust the seasoning and serve.

NOODLE AND LENTIL SOUP
(Rishta)
Follow the rice and lentil recipe, but replace the rice with ½ cup of fine pasta such as vermicelli.

EGG AND LEMON SOUP

Serves 4 to 6

This soup is popular all over the Middle East. Egg yolks are used as a thickening agent in the soup, and once they have been added it should not be allowed to boil or the yolks will curdle. For a thinner soup halve the quantity of rice. On a hot day the soup can be served chilled and garnished with chopped fresh mint rather than parsley. One half pound chopped spinach can also be added at the same time as the stock.

2 tablespoons vegetable oil	salt and black pepper
1 medium onion, diced	2 egg yolks
¼ cup rice, washed and drained	juice of 1 medium or 2 small lemons
4½ cups chicken stock or water and stock cube	1 tablespoon chopped fresh parsley

Heat the oil in a heavy pan and sauté the onion until it is lightly browned. Stir in the rice and sauté over a moderate heat for 1–2 minutes. Add the stock and season to taste with salt and pepper. Bring to the boil, reduce the heat, and simmer until the rice is cooked. Remove from the heat. Beat the egg yolks and lemon juice together in a bowl and slowly stir some of the soup into it. Blend this mixture thoroughly and return it to the rest of soup. Carefully reheat the soup and keep stirring until it thickens, not allowing it to come to the boil. Adjust the seasoning, and serve the soup garnished with parsley.

HARIRA WITH LAMB AND CHICKEN
MOROCCO

Serves 8 to 10

Harira is a Moroccan soup made from mutton or lamb, vegetables, chick-peas, and grains. It is eaten all year round but traditionally each day of Ramadan at sunset. Ramadan, the ninth month of the Islamic calendar, is a time when all practicing Moslems fast from sunrise to sunset and the first meal of the day needs to be substantial.

For devout Moslems the *harira* is prepared without meat during Ramadan, and a recipe for meatless chick-pea *harira* follows this one.

4 tablespoons olive or sesame seed oil or butter

1 pound stewing lamb or mutton, cut into large cubes

1 small boiling chicken, cut into 8 pieces

2 cloves garlic, put through a garlic press

2 medium onions, finely chopped

½ cup chick-peas, soaked overnight and drained or 8-ounce can cooked chick-peas, drained

8 cups water or stock

½ teaspoon each turmeric, powdered ginger, coriander seeds, and cinnamon

salt and black pepper to taste

1 pound ripe tomatoes, quartered

½ cup lentils, washed

2 tablespoons finely chopped parsley

¼ cup rice, washed

2 beaten eggs

juice of 1 lemon

lemon wedges

cayenne or hot pepper sauce

In a large heavy frying pan heat the oil or butter and lightly brown the lamb or mutton cubes on all sides. Transfer them to a large pan and repeat for the chicken pieces, garlic, and onions. Add the chick-peas and water or stock to the pan. Stir in the spices, salt, pepper, tomatoes, and lentils. Bring to the boil, cover, reduce the heat, and simmer for 40 minutes. Add the parsley and rice and cook a further 20 minutes. Remove the chicken pieces from the pan. Skin them, separate the meat from the bones, and put the meat back in the pot. Adjust the seasoning and bring to the boil again. Reduce the heat and set to simmer. Whisk the beaten eggs and lemon juice together and slowly whisk it into the soup to form strands of egg. Serve the soup immediately with lemon wedges and cayenne or hot pepper sauce for those who like hot dishes.

CHICK-PEA HARIRA
MOROCCO

Serves 6 to 8

1¼ cups chick-peas, soaked overnight and drained

1 diced medium onion

¼ cup butter or vegetable oil

1 small bunch parsley, finely chopped

½ teaspoon turmeric or saffron

1 teaspoon ground cinnamon

salt and black pepper

½ cup rice, washed

3 tablespoons flour

2 eggs, lightly beaten (optional)

juice of 1 lemon

Put the chick-peas, onion, butter or oil, parsley, turmeric or saffron, and cinnamon ingredients into a heavy pot and stir over a medium heat for 3–4 minutes. Add 8 cups water and bring to the boil. Cover, reduce the heat, and simmer until the chick-peas are cooked (about 1 hour). Season to taste with salt and pepper and add the rice. Return to the boil, reduce the heat, and simmer until the rice is cooked (about 25–30 minutes). Now, beat the flour and ¾ cup water into a smooth paste and stir into the soup. Continue cooking, stirring occasionally, for a further 15 minutes and then remove the soup from the heat. Adjust the seasoning, add water if needed, and, if you wish, stir in the lightly beaten eggs, which will form strands and thicken the soup. Add the lemon juice and leave the soup to stand for a few minutes or until the egg is cooked.

EGYPTIAN GREEN HERB SOUP
(Melokhia)

Serves 6 to 8

Melokhia is a very popular soup in Egypt, made by rich and poor alike, and with a history dating back as far as the pyramids. *Melokhia* is a green leafy vegetable similar to spinach (which could be substituted). It is unavailable fresh in the West, but a dried variety that makes a good alternative is available in grocery shops selling Middle Eastern ingredients. The soup is made with chicken stock and served with sliced boiled chicken and boiled rice. Preceding the *melokhia* recipe is a recipe for preparing the chicken stock and boiled chicken used in its preparation.

CHICKEN STOCK AND MEAT

1 boiling chicken, 3–4 pounds
2 leeks or onions, chopped
2 cloves garlic
1 pound ripe tomatoes, skinned and quartered

2 sticks celery and leaves
salt and coarsely ground black pepper
10 cups water

Put all the ingredients into a large pot and bring to the boil. Reduce the heat, cover, and simmer for 2–3 hours or until the chicken is tender. Skim the surface of the liquid from time to time. Remove the chicken, strain the stock, and return the stock to the pot. Adjust the seasoning. Skin and bone the chicken, cut up the meat, and reserve.

PREPARING THE MELOKHIA

4 ounces dried melokhia or 2 pounds
  fresh melokhia (or spinach), very
  finely chopped
chicken stock from recipe above
4 cloves garlic
¼ teaspoon salt

2 tablespoons melted butter
1 teaspoon ground coriander
pinch of cayenne
cooked chicken
boiled rice

Crumble the dried *melokhia* in a bowl and just cover it with warm water. Leave it to double in bulk. Bring the stock to the boil and add the prepared *melokhia* or the chopped fresh leaves. Mix well and leave to simmer for 20–30 minutes (½ this time for the fresh leaves). Stir now and again to prevent the leaves from sinking in the pan. Now put the garlic through a garlic press and mix it with the salt. Heat the butter in a small pan and add the garlic and the salt mixture. Gently cook until the garlic is nicely browned. Stir in the coriander and cayenne and heat them through. Add this mixture to the soup and stir well. Heat to boiling, remove from the heat, and serve with slices of the cooked chicken and rice.

KISHK SOUP
(Shurabat al Kishk)
SYRIA

Serves 4

This soup, popular in Syria and Lebanon, is eaten at any time of the day. *Kishk* itself is made by combining cracked wheat (burghul), yogurt and milk, and various spices and allowing the mixture to ferment. This is then dried in the sun and crushed to a dry powder. *Kishk* may be hard to find but Middle East specialty stores do stock it.

2 tablespoons olive oil or melted butter
2 cloves garlic, put through a garlic
  press
1 large onion, finely diced
4 ounces kishk
3 cups water or stock

salt and black pepper to taste
2 eggs, hard-boiled, shelled, and
  chopped
2 tablespoons finely chopped parsley

Put the oil or butter in a pan, add the garlic and onion, and gently sauté until softened. Stir in the *kishk* and add the water or stock and seasoning. Stir constantly until the soup is thick and just boiling. It should be creamy and smooth. Serve in individual bowls and garnish with chopped egg and parsley.

VARIATION: Cook ½ pound lean ground lamb along with the garlic and onion and then proceed as directed in the recipe.

MEATBALL SOUP
(Kufta Soup)
FERTILE CRESCENT

This soup can be made in a variety of ways, so I have given a recipe for making the meatballs, followed by recipes for their use in a chicken stock soup and then a lamb stock soup. You may of course add meatballs to any soup that you wish to make more substantial.

MEATBALLS

1 pound finely ground lamb, mutton, or beef	2 tablespoons finely chopped parsley
½ teaspoon ground cinnamon	1 egg, beaten
½ teaspoon ground allspice	salt and black pepper to taste
	oil for frying

Combine all the ingredients except the oil and knead the mixture vigorously, by hand or with a food processor, into a smooth paste. Form into 1-inch balls and fry them in ¼–½ inch of oil until just browned.

VARIATIONS: Add ground almonds, raisins, or lemon juice to the ingredients.

CHICKEN STOCK AND MEATBALL SOUP

Serves 6

5 cups chicken stock (for preparation see
  melokhia *soup recipe above*)
meatballs as prepared above, fried

2 eggs
juice of 2 lemons
ground cinnamon

Heat the chicken stock to boiling, then reduce the heat to simmer. Drop in the meatballs, cover, and leave them to simmer for 30 minutes. Reduce the heat to below simmering. Beat the eggs with the lemon juice and slowly pour this into the soup. Gently whisk as you do it to form strands of egg. Serve garnished with a light sprinkling of cinnamon.

LAMB STOCK AND MEATBALL SOUP

Serves 6

7 cups water
2 lamb shanks (knuckles)
1 small onion, diced
½ teaspoon cinnamon

salt and black pepper to taste
meatballs as prepared above, fried
½ cup rice, washed

Put the water, lamb shanks, onion, cinnamon, and seasoning in a pot. Bring it to the boil, reduce the heat, cover, and simmer for 1 hour or until the meat on the bone is cooked. Remove the scum from the surface as it forms. Add the meatballs and continue to simmer for 30 minutes. At 15 minutes before the end of cooking time add the rice. Finally remove the shanks and cut off any meat. Return the meat to the pot. Adjust the seasoning and serve.

YEMENI LAMB SOUP

Serves 8

A filling and colorful soup.

1 cup chick-peas or other beans or brown lentils, soaked overnight, drained
1 pound stewing lamb, cubed
2 pounds lamb bones, washed
2 cloves garlic, put through a garlic press
1 medium onion, chopped
2 medium carrots, chopped

2 tablespoons oil
8 ounces ripe tomatoes, skinned and chopped
1 teaspoon caraway seeds
½ teaspoon cardamom
1 teaspoon turmeric
salt and black pepper to taste
parsley, finely chopped

Put the chick-peas or beans, 7 cups water, lamb, and bones in a large pot, bring it to a boil, cover, reduce the heat, and simmer for 2 hours or until the beans and meat are tender. Remove any scum as it forms. Sauté the garlic, onion, and carrots in the oil until the onion is softened. Stir the tomatoes, spices, and seasoning into the onion mixture. Heat through and then add the mixture to the lamb and beans pot. Continue to cook until the vegetables are cooked. Remove the bones and serve the soup garnished with chopped parsley.

ARAB FISH SOUP

Serves 6

1 pound cod, halibut, haddock, or other white fish
salt and black pepper to taste
1 teaspoon ground coriander
2 tablespoons butter or olive oil

1 tablespoon flour
1 egg, beaten
juice of 1 lemon
wedges of lemon
parsley, finely chopped

Cut the fish into 4 pieces and put them in a pot with 5 cups water. Season to taste with salt and pepper and add the coriander. Simmer until the fish is tender. Remove the fish, bone it, and return the flesh to the pot. Heat the butter or oil in a small pan and stir in the flour; add a little fish stock to form a smooth paste. Add the egg and lemon juice to the flour mixture, and more fish stock to make a smooth sauce. Pour this back into the soup and heat through. Serve with wedges of lemon and garnish with chopped parsley.

Breads, Pies and Savory Pastries

Basic Pita Bread

Seasoned Pita Bread

Pizza Sandwich

Arabian Meat Pizza

Open Meat Pies

Open Vegetable Pies

Open Meat and Vegetable Pie

Triangle Spinach Pies

Quick Spiced Onion Bread

Unyeasted Arab Bread

Fried Egg Pastries

Lamb and Cheese Pastries

Chicken Pastries

Shortcrust Pastry Dough

Flaky Pastry Dough

Cheese Filling

Lamb Filling

Vegetable Filling

*W*heat is a staple cereal of the fertile areas surrounding the deserts of Arabia, and bread made from wheat flour is an intrinsic part of every Arabic meal.

Aish (Egypt), *khoubiz* (Gulf States), *kesra* (Algeria), *kmaj* (Lebanon), or pita bread as we know it best in the West are all varieties of the most common type of Arabic bread. This is a slightly leavened, flat, and usually round-shaped bread with a soft crust and a hollow or pocket running along the inside. The bread is cooked in a variety of ways, but the basic principle is to provide a very hot oven or other baking source (e.g., a metal dome or *sorj* heated over an open fire until very hot, over which the bread dough is draped to bake) in which the bread is baked for a short period at a high temperature. This type of bread does not keep fresh for very long and needs to be made the day it is to be eaten. Arab bakers bake morning and evening. However, it does freeze successfully, and if you bake any at home you can freeze the unused bread for later use. To reuse, put the frozen bread straight into a very hot oven for 5–8 minutes.

During a meal pieces of bread are used to scoop up food or folded double and used to pick up a tempting morsel. The hollow in the bread also provides a convenient pouch for filling with food and making a sort of Arabic sandwich.

Apart from the type with a pocket there are unyeasted Arabic flat breads, and a recipe for a bread of this type is given below, along with various methods for baking regular pita bread topped with vegetable or meat sauces.

Small pies made with bread dough cases, and savory pastries made with shortcrust, puff, or fila pastry are great favorites of the Arab world. They are made in a bewildering array of shapes and sizes and given a confusing range of names. To make things easier for the Western cook I have selected a small number of uncomplicated and well-tried recipes which nevertheless give a true taste of this fascinating side of Arabic cooking. They can be served hot or cold as hors d'oeuvre (mezze), snacks, and buffet dishes or as part of a main course.

BASIC PITA BREAD
(Khoubiz-Arabi)
LEBANON

Makes 8 loaves (allow ½ loaf per person)

1 ounce fresh yeast or ½ ounce dried
   yeast
pinch of sugar
about 2 cups warm water

4 cups plain flour
1 teaspoon salt
2 tablespoons oil (olive oil if possible)

In a small bowl mix the yeast, sugar, and 4 tablespoons of the warm water into a smooth paste and set aside in a warm place for 10–15 minutes or until the mixture has frothed up. Put the flour and salt in a deep mixing bowl, make a well in the center, and pour in the yeast mixture, remaining water, and oil. Knead the mixture into a smooth dough. If it is too hard add a little more water or if too soft a little more flour.

Turn the dough onto a lightly floured board and knead by hand for about 15 minutes. The final dough should be smooth and elastic. Put the dough in a lightly oiled bowl, cover with a damp cloth, and leave in a warm place for 1½–2 hours.

Turn the dough onto a floured board, punch it down, and divide it into 8 equal portions. Roll these into balls and roll each ball out into an 8–10-inch round loaf. Leave them to rest on a floured surface, covered with a cloth, for 20 minutes.

Place a large baking sheet on the top shelf of a gas oven or the lowest shelf of an electric oven and preheat the oven to 500° F. Now remove the baking sheet and carefully, with a wad of paper or a brush, lightly grease the top surface. Using two floured spatulas, lift one of the loaves onto the baking sheet and then, if there's room, a second. Bake the bread in the oven for 5 minutes or until it puffs up and turns a delicate brown in color. Remove it from the oven and keep it warm in a cloth while you repeat the process for the other loaves.

RECIPES USING PITA
BREAD DOUGH

The following breads and pies are made using the same dough as prepared above. They may be made separately or you may wish to keep back some prepared pita dough and use it to try out these variations on the basic bread.

SEASONED PITA BREAD
(Mraquish biz Zatar)
LEBANON

Makes 2 loaves

2 round uncooked pita loaves   2 tablespoons zatar
olive oil

Flute the edges of the loaves with your fingertips and then brush the tops with olive oil. Sprinkle the *zatar* over the loaves and spread it evenly, making finger indentations in the dough as a pattern. Bake the loaves in the same way as basic pita bread. You may wish to experiment with this recipe, using herbs and spices other than those suggested.

Zatar is a herb mixture that includes thyme, marjoram, and *sumak* (the lemony-flavored dried berries of the *sumak* tree). It is not readily available in the United States, but a good substitute can be made by mixing 1 teaspoon each of crushed thyme, crushed marjoram, and freshly grated lemon rind.

PIZZA SANDWICH
(Khoubiz bij-Jibin)
FERTILE CRESCENT

1 baked pita loaf per person   salt and freshly ground black pepper
tomatoes, sliced   olives
cheese, grated   oregano

Preheat the oven to 450° F. Cut a pita bread around the circumference so that you can open it up as two circles joined by a hinge of bread. Layer one side with tomato slices, cover these with grated cheese, and season with salt and pepper. Decorate with olives, sprinkle on oregano, and then fold the empty half of the bread over the top. Prepare one pizza sandwich per person and then bake them in the hot oven for 5 minutes or until the cheese has melted.

ARABIAN MEAT PIZZA
(Lahma bi-ajeen)

Serves 8

pita bread dough (page 52)
2 tablespoons olive oil
1 pound ground lamb or beef
1½ cups thinly sliced onions
1 pound fresh tomatoes, chopped
2 tablespoons tomato purée

1 teaspoon allspice
3 tablespoons finely chopped parsley
pinch of cayenne pepper
salt and black pepper to taste

Prepare the pita bread dough in the quantity given in the basic pita bread recipe and set aside to rise. Meanwhile prepare the topping: cook the meat in the oil in a heavy frying pan, stirring frequently. Just as it starts to brown add the onions and cook, stirring, until they are just soft. Add all the other ingredients and simmer over low heat, stirring occasionally, until the mixture is cooked but still quite moist (rather than sloppy). Roll out the dough on a floured surface into eight 8–10-inch flat rounds, cover them with a dry cloth, and leave them to rise for 20 minutes. Preheat the oven to 450° F. Now liberally cover each dough round with the topping and slip them one or two at a time onto lightly greased baking sheets. Bake in the oven for 8–10 minutes. If your oven only accommodates 4 at a time, keep the cooked pizzas warm on top of the oven.

OPEN MEAT PIES
(Sfiha)
JORDAN

Makes about 15 pies

pita bread dough (page 52)
1 pound lamb or beef, finely ground
1 large onion, finely diced
1 cup pine nuts, lightly toasted in the oven (chopped walnuts can be substituted)

2 tablespoons finely chopped parsley (optional)
pinch of cinnamon
juice of 1 lemon
salt and black pepper to taste
butter, melted
yogurt

Follow the basic pita bread dough recipe, using 50 percent of all ingredients, but 100 percent yeast, and leave to rise for 1½–2 hours. Combine the remaining ingredients (except butter and yogurt) and mix them well together. Roll out the risen dough on a floured board until about ¼-inch thick. Cut into 6-inch circles and brush each circle with melted butter. Preheat the oven to 400° F. Place a heaped tablespoon of filling in the center of each round and bring up the edges to form a lip around the mixture. As you make them put them onto a greased baking sheet. Bake for 20–25 minutes or until very lightly browned. Serve with a bowl of plain yogurt which can be spooned over the pies before eating.

VARIATIONS: A variation on the above recipe is to replace the lemon juice with ½ cup of yogurt.

This filling can also be used in place of the spinach filling of the spinach pie recipe below to make triangle meat pies (*ftayir*).

OPEN VEGETABLE PIES

Makes about 15 pies

Follow the meat pie recipe above, but use the following filling:

1 large onion, finely diced	pinch of cinnamon and nutmeg
2 tablespoons vegetable or olive oil	1 cup pine nuts, lightly toasted in the
2 medium green bell peppers, seeded	oven (chopped walnuts can be sub-
and deribbed, finely chopped	stituted)
2 medium red bell peppers, seeded and	juice of 1 lemon
deribbed, finely chopped	salt and black pepper to taste
2 tablespoons finely chopped parsley	

Sauté the onion in 2 tablespoons of oil until it is just softened, add the green and red peppers, and continue cooking until they are just soft. Combine this mixture with the remaining oil and all other ingredients and mix well. Proceed as in the recipe above.

OPEN MEAT AND VEGETABLE PIE

Make half the quantities of each of the meat and vegetable fillings given above, combine them and mix well, and use to make the open pies (*sfiha*) described in the open meat pie recipe above.

TRIANGLE SPINACH PIES
(Sbanikh bil-Ajn)
FERTILE CRESCENT

Makes 30–40 pies

pita bread dough (page 52)
1½ pounds spinach, washed, finely chopped
2 medium onions, finely chopped
½ cup olive oil

¼ teaspoon allspice
¾ cup raisins (optional)
juice of 2 lemons
salt and black pepper to taste

Follow the basic pita bread dough recipe, using 50 percent of all ingredients but 100 percent of the yeast, and leave to rise for 1½–2 hours. Cook the spinach in a large heavy pan until it is wilted, then drain it in a colander to remove the juices. Press the spinach with the back of a wooden spoon to ensure it is as dry as possible. Cook the onions in the oil in a large frying pan until softened and then add the spinach and cook, stirring for 5 minutes. Add the remaining ingredients, mix well, and cook over low heat for another 5 minutes. Leave to cool.

Roll out the risen dough on a floured board until about ¼ inch thick. Cut into 4-inch rounds. Cover them with a floured cloth. Being careful not to wet the edges, spoon a tablespoon of filling onto the center of each round. Bring up the circumference at three points so as to form a three-sided pyramid or triangle shape and then press the edges together to seal them. Preheat the oven to 400° F. Bake the pies on a greased baking sheet in the oven for about 20 minutes or until lightly browned.

VARIATION: Any of the fillings used in the open pie recipes may be substituted for the spinach in this recipe, and vice versa.

QUICK SPICED ONION BREAD
(Khoubiz Basali)
SYRIA

Makes 8 flat rounds

This is a Syrian bread using baking powder as the raising agent. It has a distinctive taste that goes well with cheese.

3½ cups self-rising flour	½ teaspoon ground cumin
2 teaspoons baking powder	½ teaspoon ground coriander
pinch of salt	¼ teaspoon or more cayenne
1 medium onion, finely chopped	4 tablespoons olive oil
1 teaspoon dried thyme	plain flour

Sift the flour, baking powder, and salt into a bowl. Add the onion, thyme, cumin, coriander, cayenne, and oil and mix well. Make a hollow in the mixture and add 2 cups water slowly to form a smooth soft dough that doesn't stick to the sides of the bowl. Flour a working surface and knead the dough for 10 minutes or more. Divide the dough into 8 and roll each into a flat round about ¼ inch thick. Dust each with flour and cover with a dry cloth. Leave for 30 minutes to rise. Preheat the oven to 500° F. Place 2 lightly greased baking trays in the oven for 5 minutes after the oven is hot. Put the bread on the trays and bake for 8–10 minutes or until the tops are lightly browned. Remove from the oven and allow to cool before using.

UNYEASTED ARAB BREAD
(Khobz)
YEMEN

Makes 8 rounds

This bread is unyeasted and it is cooked on top of the stove in a large frying pan. No baking is required.

3½ cups whole-wheat flour	¾ cup lukewarm water
1 level teaspoon salt	vegetable oil

Combine the flour and salt and add the water. Mix well and knead into a smooth dough. The longer you knead the dough the better; 10 minutes is the minimum time required. Put the dough in a bowl, cover with a damp cloth, and leave in a warm place for 2–3 hours. Now pinch off slightly larger than golf-ball size pieces of dough and form them into balls. Roll them out on a lightly floured board to form rounds of about 6 inches diameter. Cover the rounds with a dry cloth and leave for 30 minutes. Grease a heavy frying pan very lightly with vegetable oil and heat it over a medium flame. Cook the rounds in the pan one at a time for about 1–2 minutes on each side or until they are nicely browned. After half of them have been cooked, regrease the pan very lightly, using a cloth dipped in oil. Store the cooked bread rounds in a warm oven until they are all made, or, if you want to make the bread a few hours before using it, heat it just before serving.

SAVORY PASTRIES

I have divided the savory pastry recipes into two parts: those made with fila pastry and those made with shortcrust or flaky pastry. The former are always deep fried and the latter oven baked or deep fried. The fillings given for the fila pastries (except the fried egg) can be used with the shortcrust and flaky pastries and vice versa.

Savory Fila Pastries

For details of how to make or buy fila pastry and of how to use it, see page xxi. Each recipe makes 4 pastries.

FRIED EGG PASTRIES
(Brik)
NORTH AFRICA

4 sheets fila pastry
4 tablespoons butter, melted
4 small eggs
1 small onion, finely diced

1 tablespoon finely chopped parsley
salt and black pepper
oil for deep frying
lemon quarters

Brush each sheet of fila pastry with melted butter and fold it into a 5-inch square. Break one egg into the center of each square and sprinkle over it some onion, parsley, and salt and pepper to taste. Fold one corner of the square to the other to form a triangle and seal the edges. Use more melted butter if needed to get a good seal. Repeat for each sheet of fila pastry. Heat the oil to 400°F and deep fry the pastries one at a time, turning once, until golden brown (about 2–3 minutes). Drain on absorbent paper and serve with wedges of lemon.

VARIATION: The pastries may also be shallow fried in a heavy frying pan.

LAMB AND CHEESE PASTRIES
TUNISIA

The filling for these pastries can be made 3–4 hours before the pastries are prepared.

½ pound finely minced lamb
1 small onion, finely chopped
1 tablespoon finely chopped parsley
salt and black pepper to taste
2 tablespoons olive oil
1 cup grated cheese (Cheddar, Cheshire,
  or Gruyère)

4 sheets fila pastry
butter, melted
oil for deep frying
lemon quarters

To make the filling, combine the lamb, onion, parsley, salt, and pepper and mix well. Heat the oil in a heavy frying pan and fry the filling until the meat is just browned. Use a spatula to press the mixture and so prevent lumps from forming. Stir in the cheese and leave the mixture to cool.

Brush each sheet of fila pastry with melted butter and fold it into a 5-inch square. Spoon a quarter of the filling into the center of each square and fold one corner of the square to the opposite corner to form a triangle. Seal the edges, using more melted butter if it is needed to obtain a good seal. Repeat for each sheet of fila pastry.

Heat the oil to 400° F and deep fry the pastries one at a time, turning once, until golden brown. Drain on absorbent paper and serve with wedges of lemon.

VARIATIONS: The pastries may also be shallow fried in a heavy frying pan.

A small egg may be broken into the middle of each pastry before it is folded into a sealed triangle.

CHICKEN PASTRIES
IRAQ

The filling for these pastries can be made 3–4 hours before the pastries are prepared.

2 tablespoons oil
1 cup finely diced cooked chicken
1 small onion, finely chopped
½ teaspoon turmeric
½ teaspoon ground coriander
salt and black pepper

1 small egg, beaten
4 sheets fila pastry
butter, melted
oil for deep frying
lemon quarters

Heat 2 tablespoons oil in a heavy frying pan, add the chicken, onion, spices, salt, and black pepper to taste, and cook, stirring, until the onion is soft. Remove from the heat and stir in the beaten egg. The filling is now ready for use. Follow exactly the same procedure as for lamb and cheese pastries (preceding recipe).

Savory Shortcrust and Flaky Pastries

The recipes are divided into three sections. First prepare the shortcrust or flaky pastry as described. (Shop-bought frozen puff pastry may be substituted.) Second, select one of the fillings and prepare this as specified. Finally, make up the pastries using the chosen filling and pastry and bake them using the method given. If desired, the shortcrust or flaky pastry dough and the filling can be prepared 3–4 hours in advance and made up into pastries just before baking.

SHORTCRUST PASTRY DOUGH

3½ cups plain flour
½ teaspoon salt

1 cup margarine or butter
2 eggs, lightly beaten

Sift the flour and salt into a mixing bowl. Cut the margarine or butter into the bowl, and either rub it into the flour with your hands or use an electric beater. Add the eggs and mix them in with your fingers. Continue working the dough and slowly add enough water to form a soft ball that does not stick to the sides of the bowl. Cover the bowl with a damp cloth and set aside for 1 hour in a cool place. The dough is now ready to use.

FLAKY PASTRY DOUGH

3½ cups plain flour
1 teaspoon salt
4 tablespoons olive oil or other vegetable
  oil

juice of 1 lemon
about 2 cups iced water
1 cup margarine or butter

Sift the flour and salt into a large bowl and add the oil and lemon juice. Knead in enough iced water to form a soft dough. Roll the dough on a floured board into a rectangle about 2 by 8 inches. Spread the margarine or butter over the top, fold the pastry into three, then place it in the refrigerator for 30 minutes. Remove it and roll the dough into the same size rectangular shape as before, but this time roll across the dough at right angles to the first direction of rolling. Fold into three again and refrigerate for 30 minutes. Repeat twice more, changing the rolling direction each time. After the final 30 minutes' refrigeration the pastry is ready for use.

Fillings The quantities given for the following fillings make enough to use up the quantity of pastry prepared in either one of the recipes given above, to serve 8–10 people. Each filling yields approximately 30 pastries.

CHEESE FILLING

1 pound mature Cheddar, grated
8 ounces feta cheese, crumbled
2 teaspoons dried mint or 2 tablespoons
   finely chopped fresh mint

2 eggs, beaten
pinch of allspice
salt and black pepper to taste

Combine all the ingredients and mix well.

LAMB FILLING

2 tablespoons butter
2 cloves garlic, put through a garlic
   press
1 pound lamb, ground
1 large onion, finely chopped

¾ cup pine nuts, lightly toasted, or
   chopped walnuts
pinches of allspice and cinnamon
salt and black pepper to taste

Melt the butter in a heavy frying pan, add the garlic, and gently sauté. Add the lamb and fry, stirring, until lightly browned. Add the onion, nuts, and spices and cook until the onion is softened. Season to taste with salt and pepper and leave to cool.

VEGETABLE FILLING

1 medium onion, finely chopped
2 tablespoons butter
2 medium red peppers, seeded, deribbed
   and finely chopped
2 medium zucchini, coarsely grated

12 ounces spinach, washed, stalks cut
   away, finely chopped
ground cinnamon
salt and black pepper
1 egg, lightly beaten

In a heavy pan sauté the onion in the butter until the onion is just softened. Add the peppers, zucchini, and spinach and cook until the vegetables are just soft and the spinach is wilted. Season to taste with cinnamon, salt, and pepper and remove from the heat. Leave it for a few minutes and then stir in the beaten egg. Leave to cool.

VARIATION: Add 2 tablespoons raisins and/or ½ cup grated cheese.

Preparing Savory Shortcrust Pastries   On a floured board roll out the prepared shortcrust pastry dough (page 61) as thin as possible. Cut it into 4-inch squares or circles. Put a full teaspoonful of filling into the center of each and fold the squares into triangles and the circles into half moons. Seal the edges well together, using a little milk or water if needed, and then pattern them with your finger or a fork. Transfer the filled pastries to an ungreased baking tray. Brush the tops with egg beaten with a little water, and bake the pastries in a preheated oven at 350° F for about 40 minutes or until golden brown.

Preparing Savory Flaky Pastries   Roll out the prepared flaky pastry dough (page 61) as thin as possible. Cut it into 4-inch squares or circles, and put a full teaspoon of selected savory filling in the center of each. Fold the squares into triangles and the circles into half circles, and press or pinch the edges together to seal them. Put the filled pastries on an ungreased baking tray and brush them with egg mixed with a little water. Bake them in a preheated oven at 375° F for 30 minutes or until golden brown (sometimes the pastries are sprinkled with sesame seeds before being put in the oven). Alternatively, deep fry the pastries in hot oil and then drain them on absorbent paper.

Salads

Mixed Salad

Toasted Bread and Salad

Potato Salad

Potato and Green Bean Salad

Spicy Potato and Caraway Seed Salad

Tomato Salad

Moroccan Orange and Carrot Salad

Zucchini Salad

Lebanese Eggplant Salad

Algerian Eggplant Salad

Moroccan Tomato and Pepper Salad

Orange and Onion Salad

Orange and Radish Salad

Orange and Olive Salad

Moroccan Orange and Date Salad

Fried Apple, Pepper, and Tomato Salad

Spiced Burghul Wheat Salad

Lentil Salad

Spinach and Walnut Salad

Spinach and Bean Salad

Pickled Vegetables

Salads can accompany any Arabic meal from breakfast to supper. They are made from combinations of a wide variety of vegetables, legumes, and fruits dressed with liberal amounts of olive oil, lemon juice, and sometimes garlic. They are seasoned with salt and black pepper and in North African countries with cayenne, and garnished with olives and any fresh herbs available, e.g. parsley, mint, coriander leaves, chives, and so on. Where you can, choose fresh, crisp vegetables for the salads and if you are making a cooked vegetable salad leave the vegetables with some texture—do not overcook them. After adding the dressing leave the salad to marinate in it for a short while before serving.

For me, salads rich in olive oil and lemon juice are the easiest way to transport a flavor of the Middle East to the Western table. I hope the following recipes provide you with a few new ideas.

MIXED SALAD

Chopped or sliced raw vegetables served with olive oil, lemon juice, salt, pepper, and lots of fresh herbs are the basis of the everyday Arab salad. I have not given fixed amounts in this recipe, just a general outline within which you can work.

tomatoes, quartered
cucumber, sliced or cut in sticks
cooked beets, sliced
lettuce leaves, chopped
scallions, chopped
mild onion, sliced
olive oil
lemon juice
salt and black pepper
fresh and finely chopped herbs, e.g.: mint, parsley, basil, dill, coriander, etc.

Arrange the vegetables in a bowl, pour plenty of olive oil and lemon juice over them, season, and sprinkle with a generous amount of fresh herbs. If you can wait, leave the salad for 5 minutes before serving.

TOASTED BREAD AND SALAD
(Fattoush)
SYRIA

Serves 4 to 6

Fattoush means "moistened bread," and this salad consists of a chilled mixed salad tossed with small cubes of toasted bread. The texture of the toasted bread adds an unusual quality.

2 or 3 tomatoes, cubed
1 small cucumber, peeled, quartered lengthwise, and chopped
1 medium green pepper, seeded, deribbed, and diced
5 scallions, chopped
½ small lettuce, shredded
2 tablespoons finely chopped parsley
1 tablespoon finely chopped fresh mint or 1 teaspoon dried mint

1 pita bread (or 2–3 slices of bread), toasted and cut into cubes
a dressing made from equal amounts of olive oil and lemon juice and seasoned with salt and black pepper. (Make plenty of dressing and store whatever you do not use in the fridge.)

Combine the vegetables, herbs, and bread. Make the dressing, pour it over the salad, toss well, and chill for 30–60 minutes before serving. For an authentic Arabic flavor, the dressing should be made of equal parts of oil and lemon juice. However, you may prefer to use more oil— perhaps two to three parts of oil to one of lemon juice.

POTATO SALAD
LEBANON

Serves 6

2 pounds potatoes
salt
1 medium onion, finely diced
3 tablespoons finely chopped parsley
1 tablespoon finely chopped fresh mint or 1 teaspoon dried mint

2 cloves garlic, crushed
1 tablespoon lemon juice
3 tablespoons olive oil
salt and black pepper to taste

Scrub the potatoes and boil them in their jackets in plenty of salted water until they are just tender. Do not overcook. Drain them and as soon as they are cool enough, peel off the skins. Cut the potatoes into small cubes and combine them with the onion, parsely, and mint. Mix the garlic, lemon juice, olive oil, and seasoning and pour it over the salad. Toss well and serve.

POTATO AND GREEN BEAN SALAD
LEBANON

Follow the recipe above but replace the onion by ½ pound green beans. Top and tail them, cut into 2-inch lengths, and cook in a little salted water until they are almost tender but still crisp. Drain, cool, and combine them with the potatoes.

SPICY POTATO AND
CARAWAY SEED SALAD
TUNISIA

Prepare cooked potato cubes as described for potato salad (above) and toss them with a dressing made of:

4 tablespoons olive oil

2 tablespoons lemon juice

1 teaspoon finely chopped and seeded red chili pepper

2 teaspoons caraway seeds, crushed

salt to taste

TOMATO SALAD
YEMEN

Serves 6

1½ pounds firm tomatoes, sliced
1 medium onion, finely diced or small
    bunch scallions, chopped
2 tablespoons lemon juice
3 tablespoons olive oil

salt and black pepper
pinch of ground cumin (optional) and/
    or pinch of cayenne (optional)
2 tablespoons finely chopped parsley or
    coriander leaves

Arrange the tomatoes in layers on a serving dish. Sprinkle each layer with diced onion and pour, over each, part of a dressing made by combining the lemon juice, olive oil, seasoning, cumin, and/or cayenne. Sprinkle parsley or coriander leaves over the top and serve with bread.

MOROCCAN ORANGE
AND CARROT SALAD

Serves 4

½ cup raisins, soaked for 30 minutes
    in hot water
1 pound carrots, peeled and grated
1 large orange, peeled, pith removed,
    and segmented

2 tablespoons lemon juice
2 tablespoons orange juice
1 teaspoon ground cinnamon

Combine all the ingredients and mix well. Chill and serve.

ZUCCHINI SALAD
TUNISIA

Serves 6

This Tunisian salad is sometimes prepared with well-cooked, mashed zucchini, but I prefer to leave the zucchini just tender and sliced.

1½ pound zucchini, scrubbed
salt
2 cloves garlic, put through a garlic
 press
4 tablespoons olive oil

2 tablespoons lemon juice
2 teaspoons caraway seeds, crushed
pinch of cayenne
salt and black pepper to taste

Boil the zucchini in a little salted water until just tender. Drain, allow to cool a little, and then cut into ½-inch round slices. Combine the other ingredients, and pour them over the zucchini. Toss well and serve, or chill and serve later.

LEBANESE EGGPLANT SALAD

Serves 4 to 6

2 medium eggplants
3 tablespoons tahini
2 tablespoons lemon juice
2 tablespoons water

2 cloves garlic, put through a
 garlic press
salt to taste
olive oil
finely chopped parsley

Using a fork or skewer, hold the eggplants over an open gas flame or under a broiler and sear them all over until the skin is blackened and bubbly. Rub the skin off under a cold tap and place the pulp in a colander to drain off. Press it gently to remove the bitter juices. Combine the tahini, lemon juice, water, garlic, and salt and mix well. Cut the eggplants to cubes and pour the dressing over them. Serve with olive oil, parsley sprinkled over the salad to your taste, and lots of bread.

ALGERIAN EGGPLANT SALAD
(Batenjal m'charmel)

Serves 4 to 6

2 medium eggplants
2 cloves garlic, put through a garlic
 press
1 teaspoon paprika
1 teaspoon cayenne
1 teaspoon ground cumin

salt to taste
3 tablespoons olive oil
lemon juice
olive oil
finely chopped parsley
tomato wedges

Put the eggplants in a preheated oven at 400° F and bake until very tender. Leave to cool a little and then peel under cold running water. Place the pulp in a colander to drain. Press it gently to remove the bitter juices. Mash the pulp with garlic, spices, and salt. Now fry this purée in the olive oil, with constant stirring, until all the liquid is absorbed or evaporated. Place it in a serving dish, sprinkle with lemon juice, olive oil, and parsley, and decorate with tomato wedges.

MOROCCAN TOMATO AND PEPPER SALAD

Serves 6

In this salad the peppers are lightly broiled and peeled before use. The process gives them a texture and taste different from the raw vegetable (which may be used if you prefer). The dressing given for the salad is very good and full of subtle flavors. It also goes well with other salads. The chili pepper makes the salad very hot; reduce the amount specified if you prefer a milder salad.

6 medium peppers, red or green or a combination
6 medium tomatoes, sliced
1 small onion or bunch of scallions, chopped
2 tablespoons finely chopped parsley or coriander leaves
1 red chili pepper, seeded and finely chopped

4 tablespoons olive oil
2 tablespoons lemon juice or good vinegar
2 cloves garlic, put through a garlic press
1 teaspoon ground cumin
½ teaspoon sugar
salt and pepper to taste
black olives

Put the peppers one at a time on a fork or skewer, hold them over an open gas flame or under a broiler, and sear them all over until the skin blackens and cracks. Allow to cool and then peel them, remove the stalk, pith, and seeds, and cut them into strips. Put them in a serving dish and combine with the tomatoes, onion, herbs, and chili pepper. Combine all the remaining ingredients (except olives) and mix well. Pour this over the salad and toss well. Garnish with olives and serve.

VARIATION: Sometimes this salad is made with roasted tomatoes. To prepare them put the tomatoes on a baking sheet in an oven at 400° F. Bake for 20 minutes, remove them from the oven, and allow them to cool enough to handle. Peel the skins off, cut in half, squeeze out the seeds, and then chop up. Add to the salad and proceed as described above. Made in this way the salad is known as *salat meschoui*, a Tunisian specialty.

ORANGE AND ONION SALAD
MOROCCO

Serves 6

> 4 large oranges, peeled, pith removed, and sliced
> 2 medium mild onions, thinly sliced
> 2 tablespoons olive oil
>
> 2 tablespoons lemon juice or vinegar
> salt and black pepper to taste
> small pinch of cayenne
> olives to garnish

Make a nice pattern of the orange and onion slices in a serving dish. Combine the oil, lemon juice or vinegar, and seasoning, and pour it over the salad. Garnish with olives, chill for at least 1 hour, and serve.

ORANGE AND RADISH SALAD
MOROCCO

Serves 6

This Moroccan salad has a fresh, tangy, and refreshing flavor.

> 4 large oranges, peeled, pith removed, and segmented
> 1 bunch red radishes, trimmed, washed, and sliced
>
> juice of 2 lemons
> pinch of salt
> 1 teaspoon superfine sugar

Arrange the orange segments and radish slices in a bowl. Whisk together the lemon juice, salt, and sugar and pour the mixture over the salad. Chill and serve.

ORANGE AND OLIVE SALAD
MOROCCO

Serves 6

4 large oranges, peeled, pith removed,
   and segmented
½ cup black and/or green olives, pitted

salt
cayenne pepper
ground cumin

Combine all the ingredients, adding seasonings to taste, and mix well.

MOROCCAN ORANGE
AND DATE SALAD

Serves 6

½ small crisp lettuce head, washed
4 large oranges, peeled, pith removed
   and sliced
½ cup dates, pitted and chopped
¼ cup chopped, blanched, lightly
   toasted almonds

1 tablespoon orange flower water (optional)
juice of 1 lemon
1 teaspoon superfine sugar
pinch of salt
cinnamon

Separate the lettuce leaves and prepare a bed of them in a glass serving
bowl. Arrange the orange slices, dates, and almonds on top. Combine
the orange flower water, lemon juice, sugar, and salt, mix well, and pour
over the salad. Chill and sprinkle with cinnamon before serving.

FRIED APPLE, PEPPER, AND
TOMATO SALAD
IRAQ

Serves 6

This unusual salad works very well and can be made even more exotic
by the addition of finely chopped chili pepper and/or caraway seeds if
the idea appeals to you.

4 tablespoons olive oil or other vegetable oil

2 cloves garlic, put through a garlic press

2 medium eating apples, cored and quartered

1 medium onion, finely sliced

2 green peppers, seeded, deribbed, and diced

4 medium tomatoes, quartered

salt and black pepper to taste

juice of 1 lemon

2 tablespoons finely chopped parsley or mint.

Heat the oil in a large heavy frying pan and add the garlic, apples, onion, and peppers. Fry, while stirring, until they are lightly browned. Add the tomatoes and heat through. Season to taste with salt and pepper, then tip into a serving bowl. Arrange neatly and leave to cool. Sprinkle with lemon juice and fresh herbs and serve.

SPICED BURGHUL WHEAT SALAD
(Bazargan)
SYRIA

Serves 6

This burghul wheat salad is less well known than tabbouleh (see the recipe) but more to the taste of people who like spicy dishes.

1 cup burghul (cracked wheat)

4 tablespoons olive oil

1 medium onion, finely diced

2 tablespoons finely chopped parsley

½ cup pine nuts, lightly toasted, or chopped walnuts

½ cup tomato purée

2 teaspoons dried oregano

1 teaspoon ground cumin

½ teaspoon ground allspice

¼ teaspoon cayenne

salt and black pepper to taste

Cover the burghul with plenty of cold water and leave for 1 hour. Drain and squeeze out any excess water. Put half the oil in a frying pan and lightly sauté the onion. Transfer the burghul to a large mixing bowl and stir in the onion, frying oil, unused oil, and all the other ingredients. Mix well, cover, and refrigerate for 4–5 hours before serving. This salad improves if left a day or night before use.

LENTIL SALAD
NORTH AFRICA

Serves 4 to 6

2 cups green or brown lentils, washed
2 cloves
1 medium onion
2 bay leaves
2 cloves garlic
1 teaspoon grated lemon peel
1 medium onion, diced

2 tablespoons vegetable oil, preferably
    sesame seed oil
2 tablespoons lemon juice
½ teaspoon ground cumin
2 teaspoons ground coriander
salt and black pepper to taste
olives

Put the lentils in a heavy pot and cover them with water. Stick the cloves in the whole onion and add it to the pot. Add the bay leaves, garlic, and lemon peel. Bring to the boil, reduce the heat, cover, and simmer until the lentils are just tender (not disintegrating). Drain the lentils; remove and discard the onion, cloves, bay leaves, and garlic. Combine the lentils with the lemon peel, diced onion, vegetable oil, lemon juice, cumin, coriander, and salt and pepper to taste, and set the salad aside to chill and marinate for 1–2 hours. Garnish with the olives and serve.

SPINACH AND WALNUT SALAD
FERTILE CRESCENT

Serves 4 to 6

1 pound spinach, washed and chopped
    or 10-ounce frozen spinach, defrosted
    and drained
1 medium onion, finely diced
1 tablespoon olive oil

1 cup yogurt
1 clove garlic, finely chopped
2 tablespoons chopped walnuts
1 teaspoon crushed dried mint

Put the spinach and onion in a heavy pan. Cover and gently cook, with no added water, until the spinach is wilted and soft (about 10 minutes). Add the water and cook a further 5 minutes. Combine the yogurt and garlic and lightly toast the walnuts. Transfer the spinach and onion to a serving bowl, pour the yogurt over it, sprinkle on the walnuts, garnish with crushed mint, and serve hot.

SPINACH AND BEAN SALAD
YEMEN

Serves 4 to 6

Make this salad with your favorite beans.

¾ cup beans, soaked overnight, drained
4 tablespoons olive or other vegetable oil
2 medium onions, finely diced

1 pound spinach, washed and chopped, or 10-ounce package frozen spinach, defrosted and drained
salt and black pepper to taste

Cook the beans in plenty of water until they are just tender. Drain and put aside. Put the oil in a heavy frying pan and sauté the onions until just soft. Add the spinach and fry, stirring, until the spinach is well wilted and cooked. Season with salt and pepper. Add the beans, heat through, adjust the seasoning, transfer to a serving bowl, and serve hot or allow to cool and serve cold.

PICKLED VEGETABLES

Pickles are often an accompaniment to Arabic meals. However, from my experience most people in the Middle East now buy them from the wide and colorful selections they have in most Arabic towns and village markets. They can also be bought in Middle Eastern and Greek grocery shops in the West. To keep this book functional and for it to contain only recipes which people are likely to use, and because making pickles requires a lot of advance planning, I have decided to omit pickle recipes. If you would like to prepare Arabic pickles I would refer you to the excellent recipes in Claudia Roden's *A Book of Middle Eastern Food* or Tess Mallos's *The Complete Middle East Cookbook* or in my own book *Middle Eastern Vegetarian Cookery*.

Fish

Pilav Rice to Serve with
  Fish Dishes

Baked Fish with Tahini Sauce

Baked Fish with Hot Chili
  and Tahini Sauce

Baked Fish with Taratoor
  Sauce

Baked Fish with Nut Stuffing

Salt Fish or Smoked Fish in
  Tahini Sauce

Fried Fish in Tomato Sauce

Fried Fish in Spicy Zucchini
  and Tomato Sauce

Fried Fish with Yellow Rice

Barbecued Whole Fish

Barbecued Fish Kebabs

Fish and Chick-Pea Casserole

Pilav Rice and Fish Casserole

Fish and Lamb Casserole

Egyptian Fish Plaki

Fish and Burghul Wheat
  (Fish Kibbi)

*F*or the people who connect deserts and Arabs together, fish may seem an unlikely subject in a book on Arabic cooking, but most Arab countries open on to the sea and/or contain large rivers. The most common fish available are red and gray mullet, sea bream and sea bass, sole, cod, tuna, sardines, turbot, swordfish. Fish are sold fresh in the port of landing and in large inland towns but are available only salted in less accessible areas. Most Arabic fish recipes seem to be suitable for almost any type of fish, and this is the case for the majority of the recipes I have chosen for this chapter. The exceptions are where a firm, white-fleshed fish is suggested as being the most suitable for a particular recipe. The chapter is divided into baked fish, fried fish, barbecued fish, and casseroled fish recipes. The following fish can be used in most of the recipes given: trout, sole, salmon, plaice, sea bream, sea bass, herring, mackerel, cod, halibut, snapper, hake, and any salt fish that has been desalted and soaked. Fish is normally served with pilav rice, a recipe for which is given below.

PILAV RICE TO SERVE WITH FISH DISHES

Serves 4 to 6 with fish

4 tablespoons olive oil
½ teaspoon crushed saffron or 1 teaspoon turmeric
about 2 cups Basmati or long-grain
  rice, washed, and drained

salt and black pepper to taste
½ cup pine nuts
2 medium onions, sliced

Heat half the oil in a heavy frying pan, and stir in the saffron or turmeric. Measure out the rice in cupfuls and note how many there are. Stir the rice into the frying pan and fry and stir until all the rice is coated with oil and slightly tinted yellow. Remove the pan from the heat. Pour into the pan boiling water equal to 1½ volumes of the rice. Season to taste with salt and pepper. Bring to the boil, reduce the heat, cover, and simmer for 20 minutes or until all the moisture is absorbed and the rice is tender. Meanwhile fry the pine nuts in the remaining oil until they are lightly browned, add the onions, and stir-fry until they are softened. Serve the rice in a mound with the onions and pine nuts sprinkled over the top.

BAKED FISH

BAKED FISH WITH TAHINI SAUCE
FERTILE CRESCENT (IRAQ)

Serves 4

This dish can be prepared with individual fish fillets or one large fish. Both methods are given together with two recipes for tahini sauce. Sauce I contains less oil than sauce II. Sauce II contains no garlic.

4 fish fillets (firm white fish, e.g. halibut, cod, haddock) or 2–3-pound whole fish, scaled, cleaned, and washed
salt and pepper

oil
juice of 1 lemon
2 tablespoons finely chopped parsley
2 cloves garlic, put through a garlic press

Tahini Sauce I
6 tablespoons tahini
3 tablespoons water or stock
1 tablespoon olive oil

2 cloves garlic
salt and black pepper to taste

Tahini Sauce II
6 tablespoons tahini
3 tablespoons olive oil
1 tablespoon white wine vinegar

1 tablespoon water
salt and black pepper to taste

Garnish
lettuce
lemon wedges
olives

parsley sprigs
crushed cumin
coriander seeds

Preheat oven to 350° F.

To Bake Fish Fillets   Sprinkle the fillets with salt and pepper and gently fry them in a little oil until they are lightly browned. Cut out 4 pieces of foil big enough to wrap individual fillets and lightly oil them. Put a piece of fish in each and sprinkle a quarter of the lemon juice, parsley, garlic, and ½ tablespoon olive oil over each fish. Wrap up the foil and seal the edges. Bake in the oven for 20–25 minutes.

To Bake Whole Fish   Cut 2–3 incisions in the skin of the fish on both sides and then rub the fish inside and out with a mixture of salt, pepper, and oil. Set aside and leave for 1 hour. Cut out a piece of foil big enough to wrap the fish and lightly oil it. Put the fish in the foil and sprinkle over it the lemon juice, parsley, garlic, and 2 tablespoons olive oil. Wrap up the foil and seal the edges. Bake in the oven for 25–30 minutes.

To Serve the Fish   Combine all the ingredients of tahini sauce 1 or 2 and beat well together. If the sauce is too thick, stir in a little water. Gently heat the sauce through. Place the cooked fillets or whole fish on a bed of lettuce on a serving dish; surround with lemon wedges and olives. Pour the hot tahini dressing over the fish and decorate with parsley sprigs and crushed cumin and coriander seeds. Serve. This dish is also good served cold.

VARIATION: Add lightly toasted or fried chopped almonds or pine nuts to either the sauce or to the ingredients which are sprinkled over the fish before baking.

BAKED FISH WITH HOT CHILI AND TAHINI SAUCE

Prepare the fish as described in the recipe above, but put the fish in a baking dish rather than wrapped in foil. Prepare tahini sauce 1 or 2 and stir in ½ teaspoon of hot chili sauce or *harissa*. Pour the sauce over the fish in the baking dish and cover. Bake in a preheated 350° F oven for 30 minutes or until the fish is tender. Serve hot with lemon wedges and garnished with lightly fried or toasted pine nuts or almonds.

BAKED FISH WITH TARATOOR SAUCE
IRAQ

Serves 4 to 6

Taratoor sauce is sometimes made with tahini paste rather than with pine nuts or almonds. To make it this way just substitute the same amount of tahini as nuts in the recipe.

For special occasions this dish can be served in the traditional way. It takes a little time, but it's enjoyable. Cut the head and tail off the cooked and chilled fish. Skin the body and flake the flesh off the bones. Combine the flesh with a little diced onion and chopped parsley and season with salt and pepper. Put the flaked fish back on the serving dish and arrange it approximately into its original shape. Cover with *taratoor* sauce. Put the head and tail back in place and then have fun decorating your masterpiece with the garnishes suggested.

The fish could be baked and chilled 3–4 hours ahead, and the sauce prepared just before serving.

2–3-pound whole fish, scaled, cleaned
  and washed
juice of 1 lemon

salt, black pepper
2 tablespoons olive oil

Taratoor Sauce

fish stock from the baking of the fish
2 slices bread, very lightly toasted, cut
  into small squares
2 cloves garlic, put through a
  garlic press

juice of 2 lemons
2 tablespoons olive oil
1½ cups pine nuts, lightly roasted and/
  or chopped blanched almonds and/or
  ground almonds

Garnish

parsley sprigs
lemon wedges
olives

pine nuts or almonds, toasted
cucumber slices
apricot halves

Cut 2–3 incisions in the skin of the fish on both sides and rub it inside and out with lemon juice. Sprinkle with salt and pepper and set aside for 1 hour. Oil a large baking dish, put the fish in it, and pour over it the remaining oil. (If the fish is too big for the dish cut the fish in two.) Cover and bake in a preheated oven 375° F for 25–30 minutes or until the flesh easily flakes on the thickest part of the fish. Do not overcook.

Put the fish on a serving dish and chill. Reserve the cooking juices. Soak the toasted bread in these juices and combine this mixture in a blender or food processor (or pound together by hand) with the garlic, lemon juice, olive oil, and nuts. Blend to a smooth cream; add water if more liquid is needed. Pour the sauce over the chilled fish, smooth it out, and decorate with a selection from the garnishes suggested.

BAKED FISH WITH NUT STUFFING

Serves 6

Fish cooked in this way is also served with tahini or *taratoor* sauce (for preparation see above).

4-pound whole fish (e.g. sea bass) or 6 small fish (e.g. trout)
salt
¾ cup olive oil or other oil
1 medium onion, finely chopped
1 medium green pepper, seeded, de-ribbed, and finely chopped
1 cup of one or a mixture of hazelnuts, walnuts, or almonds, crushed

½ teaspoon allspice
½ teaspoon cinnamon
salt and black pepper to taste
3 tablespoons finely chopped parsley or dill
wedges of lemon

Clean and scale the fish, but leave the head and tail in place. Rinse the fish in cold water and dry. Rub with salt and one-third of the oil and set aside for 30 minutes. Preheat the oven to 400° F. Sauté the onion in another one-third of the oil until it is lightly browned. Add the green pepper, nuts, spices, and seasoning to taste, stir well, and fry until the peppers are soft. Remove from the heat and stir the parsley or dill into it. Fill the fish cavity with the stuffing and secure it in place with skewers or needle and thread. Spread the remaining oil around the bottom and sides of a baking dish and place the fish in it. Cover and bake in the preheated oven for 45 minutes or until the fish is tender. Twice during the cooking period baste the fish with any cooking juices that form. Serve with lemon wedges.

VARIATION: Eggplant—sliced, salted, pressed, and rinsed—may be used in place of the green pepper in the stuffing mixture.

FRIED FISH

SALT FISH OR SMOKED FISH
IN TAHINI SAUCE

Serves 4

Salting and drying fish has always been an important method for trans-
porting fish from the coasts of Arab countries to the inland towns and
villages. The recipe stipulates salted cod, but any type of salt fish is
suitable. For smoked fish ignore the desalting and soaking part of the
recipe. Salt fish prepared for cooking as below may be used in most of
the recipes in this chapter.

> *1 pound whole salt cod or smoked her-*   *tahini sauce I or II (see recipes above)*
>   *ring or mackerel, cut into chunks*   *garnish as for baked fish in tahini sauce*
> *2 tablespoons olive oil*   *(page 83)*

Put the salted cod in a large bowl of cold running water and leave for 1
hour. Then leave to soak in still water for 24 hours. Change the water
several times during this period. Drain the fish, skin and bone it, and
cut it into chunks. Heat the oil in a heavy drying pan and gently fry the
fish brown on all sides. Prepare the tahini sauce and pour it over the
fish in the pan. Carefully coat the fish in the sauce and heat through.
Serve with garnishes.

FRIED FISH IN TOMATO SAUCE
IRAQ

Serves 4

> *2–3-pound sea bass or other fish,*   *2 medium onions, sliced*
>   *cleaned and filleted or 4 fish fillets*   *2 cloves garlic*
> *juice of 1 lemon*   *1 teaspoon dried thyme*
> *salt and black pepper*   *1 egg, beaten*
> *1½ pounds fresh tomatoes or canned*   *flour*
>   *tomatoes, chopped*   *oil for frying*
> *4 tablespoons oil*   *chopped parsley*

Cut the fish into 4 portions and sprinkle them with lemon juice, salt, and pepper. Set them aside for 30 minutes. Plunge the fresh tomatoes into a pan of boiling water for 1 minute. Remove, allow to cool a little, then peel off the skins. Cut them in half, gently squeeze out and discard the seeds, and cut the tomato into pieces. Heat the oil in a pan and add the onions and garlic. Sauté, while stirring, until the onions are softened. Add the tomatoes, season to taste, and stir in the thyme. Cover the pan and simmer for 10–15 minutes. Dip the fish pieces in egg and lightly flour them. Fry them in ¼ inch hot oil until browned on both sides and tender. Transfer to a serving dish, cover with tomato sauce, and garnish with chopped parsley.

VARIATION: Alternatively put the fried fish in a baking dish, cover with the sauce, cover the dish, and bake in a preheated oven at 250° F for 20 minutes.

FRIED FISH IN SPICY ZUCCHINI
AND TOMATO SAUCE

Proceed as above but add 1 pound coarsely chopped zucchini and ½ teaspoon of hot pepper sauce or *harissa* along with the tomatoes. To give this dish a true North African flavor, use a lot of *harissa* and provide plenty of cold drinking water at the table.

FRIED FISH WITH YELLOW RICE
EGYPT

Serves 4

four ½-pound fish fillets
juice of 2 lemons
salt and black pepper
skin, bones, head and tails from filleting
oil for frying
2 medium onions, finely chopped

1 teaspoon ground cumin
½ teaspoon turmeric
1 teaspoon curry powder (optional)
1½ cups uncooked rice, washed and
   drained
lemon wedges

Sprinkle the fillets with lemon juice and seasoning and set aside. Put the bones, skin, head and tail of the fish in a pot with 2 cups water, bring to the boil, reduce the heat, and simmer for 30 minutes. Strain off the liquid and reserve. Fry the fish in hot shallow oil in a heavy frying pan until it is nicely browned on both sides. Lift the fish from the pan and set it aside in a low oven to keep warm. In the same pan and oil fry the onions until they are lightly browned and then stir in the cumin, turmeric, and curry powder if used. Stir in the rice and sauté it for a few minutes. Add the fish stock and enough extra water to make 3 cups liquid. Season to taste with salt and pepper. Bring it to the boil, reduce the heat, cover, and simmer until the rice is tender. Add more water if the pan dries out. Serve the rice piled on a serving dish with the fish fillets on top, and garnish with lemon wedges.

BARBECUED FISH
(Samak Meshwi)

Grilling over a charcoal or wood fire is a delicious way to cook fish. Different techniques are used in different Arab countries, but an ordinary picnic charcoal grill is perfectly suitable, and at second best but still giving good results, a stove broiler. All types of fish can be used. Firmer fish can be grilled whole or cubed, marinated and skewered. Softer fish should be left whole.

For four people, use 2–3 pounds of cod, trout, salmon, plaice, tuna, mackerel, red or gray mullet, sea bass or bream, or herring.

METHOD FOR WHOLE FISH

Wash and gut the fish, rinse, and wipe them dry. Slit the skin diagonally on both sides in 2–3 places. This prevents the skin from splitting and allows the heat in. The scales are left on—they help to keep the flesh intact and moist. Sprinkle the fish with salt, brush with oil inside and out, and if you wish stuff the cavity with crushed garlic and fresh herbs such as coriander, basil, oregano, fennel, and so on. Oil the grill and heat it. Lay the fish on the grill and cook them over the glowing embers until they are tender and flaky. Turn them once during cooking. Try to arrange the cooking time and heat so that you get a fish with soft moist interior and crispy brown skin. For serving see below.

METHOD FOR SKEWERED FISH

Fillet the fish and cut it into cubes. Make a marinade of equal amounts of olive oil and lemon juice seasoned with salt and black pepper and marinate the fish in it for an hour or two. If they are available, add chopped fresh herbs to the marinade. Skewer the fish cubes, oil the grill, lay on the skewers, and cook over the glowing embers, frequently brushing the kebabs with oil. Serve the grilled fish with olives, pickles, lemon wedges, salads, and lots of hot pita bread. Barbecued fish is also excellent served with tahini or *taratoor* sauces; see under Baked Fish, above.

BARBECUED FISH KEBABS
(Samek Kebab)
EGYPT

Please read the general instructions for barbecuing fish given above before proceeding with this recipe.

1 pound filleted firm, white fish, cut
    into ½-inch cubes or squares
3 tablespoons olive oil
3 tablespoons lemon juice
1 teaspoon ground cumin
3 or 4 bay leaves

salt and black pepper to taste
1 pound small tomatoes, halved
2 medium green or red peppers, seeded,
    deribbed, cut into 2-inch squares
pilav rice (page 81)
lemon wedges

Put the fish cubes in a bowl. Combine the olive oil, lemon juice, cumin, bay leaves, and seasoning and mix well. Pour this over the fish and leave it to marinate for 1–2 hours. Skewer (one skewer per person) the fish pieces, tomato halves, and pepper squares in an attractive pattern and place them on an oiled grill over glowing charcoal or under the broiler of a stove. Cook, turning the kebabs occasionally and basting them with marinade if they start to dry out. Serve on a bed of rice with lemon wedges.

CASSEROLED FISH

FISH AND CHICK-PEA CASSEROLE
LEBANON

Serves 4 to 6

2 pounds fish fillets (keep the bones,
   skin, heads, and tails)
juice of 3 lemons
4 tablespoons olive oil
2 medium onions, chopped
2 cloves garlic, put through a garlic
   press

2 cups cooked chick-peas
½ teaspoon crushed coriander seeds
½ teaspoon crushed caraway seeds
2 teaspoons paprika
salt and black pepper

Sprinkle the fish all over with half of the lemon juice, salt, and half of the oil. Set aside for 1 hour. Put the bones and trimmings from the fish in a pan, add 2 cups water, and bring to the boil. Reduce the heat, cover, and simmer for 1 hour. Put the remaining oil and the fish in a large shallow flameproof baking dish and, on top of the stove, gently brown the fish on both sides. Lift the fish out onto a plate and in the same oil sauté the onion and garlic until they are softened. Stir in the chick-peas, spices, and seasoning to taste. Put the fish back in the dish, pour the strained fish stock over it, bring it to the boil, cover, and leave it to simmer for 15–20 minutes or until the fish is tender. Remove from the heat and allow to cool. Sprinkle the remaining lemon juice over it, and serve. You may of course, if you wish, serve this dish hot.

VARIATIONS: This is a basic recipe for a fish casserole. You may add other vegetables or beans (cooked or parboiled) for a more substantial dish, or you may prepare it without the chick-peas for a light lunch.

PILAV RICE AND FISH CASSEROLE
SYRIA

Serves 6

The pilav rice can be made 3–4 hours before the casserole is to be prepared.

1½ pounds filleted fish
juice of 2 lemons
4 tablespoons olive oil
2 cloves garlic, put through a garlic press

2 tablespoons chopped fresh parsley
salt and black pepper
pilav rice (see page 81)
2 tablespoons pine nuts or almonds

Preheat the oven to 360° F. Put the fish in a baking dish. Combine the juice of 1 lemon, 2 tablespoons olive oil, the garlic, parsley, and seasoning to taste, and pour the mixture over the fish. Cover the dish and bake in the preheated oven for 20-25 minutes or until the fish is tender and flaky. Remove the fish and flake it into small pieces. Make a bed of half the pilav rice in the baking dish, cover with half the fish, and sprinkle with lemon juice. Repeat for another layer. Fry the pine nuts or almonds light brown in the remaining oil and then pour the nuts and oil over the contents of the dish. Bake uncovered in the hot oven for 15 minutes.

FISH AND LAMB CASSEROLE
EGYPT

Serves 4

4 tablespoons olive oil
4 fish fillets, about ½ pound each
2 cloves garlic, put through a garlic press
2 medium onions, sliced
1 pound lamb, ground
1 pound tomatoes, peeled and quartered

½ teaspoon ground cumin
1 teaspoon paprika
salt and black pepper
juice of 2 lemons
lettuce
lemon wedges

Preheat the oven to 325° F. Heat the oil in a heavy frying pan and brown the fish fillets on both sides. Lift the fish out and place them in a baking dish. In the same frying pan sauté the garlic and onion until softened. Stir in the lamb, tomatoes, spices, and seasoning to taste. Gently fry, while stirring, until the meat is browned. Pour the contents of the pan over the fish fillets and squeeze the lemon juice over them. Cover the baking dish and bake it in the preheated oven for 1½ hours. Serve with crisp lettuce and wedges of lemon.

EGYPTIAN FISH PLAKI

Serves 4

2 pounds fish, cut into 4 portions, or
    4 fish fillets
4 tablespoons olive oil
3 medium onions, sliced
3 cloves garlic, put through a garlic
    press
2 tablespoons chopped parsley or celery
    leaves

1 pound tomatoes, skinned and chopped
    or canned tomatoes, chopped
juice of 1 lemon
salt and black pepper
¾ cup raisins, covered in warm water,
    soaked 30 minutes (optional)

Preheat the oven to 350° F. Fry the fish in the oil until they are nicely browned. Transfer them to the baking dish. Fry the onions and garlic in the same oil until they are lightly browned. Add the parsley or celery leaves, tomatoes, lemon juice, and seasoning to taste. Mix well and set to simmer for 10 minutes. Add a little water or stock if the sauce gets very thick. Pour the sauce over the fish in the baking dish and top with the soaked raisins and their liquid. Bake in the preheated oven for 25 minutes or until the fish is tender.

VARIATION: This dish may be prepared with a whole fish, in which case cut 2–3 incisions in the skin of the fish on both sides and rub it inside and out with salt, pepper, and oil and set aside for 1 hour. Now proceed as directed above, except that the baking time will be a little longer.

FISH AND BURGHUL WHEAT
(Fish Kibbi)
SYRIA AND LEBANON

Serves 6 to 8

See page 138 for a discussion of *kibbi*. Serve with salad, yogurt, and bread.

1 pound fish, filleted and skinned	3 tablespoons vegetable oil, preferably
½ teaspoon ground coriander	sesame seed oil
grated skin of small orange	1 medium onion, diced
½ small onion, diced	½ cup pine nuts
salt and black pepper	¼ cup melted butter
2 cups burghul wheat, fine grade	

Preheat the oven to 350° F. Mash the fish, coriander, orange skin, and the half onion into a paste in a pestle and mortar or pass them through a grinder, blender, or food processor. Season to taste with salt and pepper. Soak the burghul in iced water for 20 minutes, drain, and squeeze dry. Mix the fish paste with the burghul and grind again. Lightly brown the other onion in the oil, add the nuts, and fry another 2–3 minutes. Grease a shallow baking dish and layer half the burghul paste on the bottom. Spread on this the onion and nut mixture and then top with the remaining paste. Brush the top with melted butter and bake for 40-45 minutes or until it is golden brown.

Meat
and
Poultry
Dishes

Lamb and Apricot Tagine

Tunisian Lamb Tagine

Kofta (Meatball) and
   Vegetable Tagine

Ground Meat with Okra

Meat Croquettes (Kofta)

Eggs in a Lamb Coat

Roasted Lamb Moroccan
   Style

Whole Roast Lamb

Stuffed Breast of Veal
   or Lamb

Arab Lamb Stew

Egyptian Beef Stew with
   Eggs

Lamb with Prunes

Lamb with Dates

Lamb with Cumin

Baked Lamb and Vegetables

Baked Lamb and Eggplant

Meat and Wheat Stew
   (Harissa)

Marinated Lamb Kebabs

Lamb with Lemon Juice

Lamb with Rice and Eggplant

Rice with Lamb Casserole

Lamb with Beans and Rice

Yemeni Beef and Rice

Skewered Liver with Garlic

Liver and Kidney Casserole

Hot Spiced Chicken with
   Lemon Juice

Yellow Chicken with
   Almonds

Grilled Chicken

Chicken with Chick-Peas

Chicken with Olives

Honey Roasted Chicken

Curried Roasted Chicken

Roast Chicken Stuffed with
   Rice

Spicy Stuffed Chicken
   Moroccan Style

Meat-Stuffed Chicken

Fried Chicken with Spinach

Chicken Tagine

Chicken, Rice, and Orange
   Pilav

Baghdad Chicken and Rice

L amb and mutton are the most common meats in the Arab diet. Sheep are most suited to the climate and pasturage available to the desert dweller. Beef, although available, is not usually very good quality, and cows are used for dairy produce or draft work. Pork is not allowed by Muslim dietary law. Lamb is cooked by many different methods, for example as a casserole with vegetables and pulses or baked or roasted or stewed, or grilled over charcoal. The dishes are always cleverly spiced and usually served with a mixture of salads, bread, and plain yogurt. Lemon, garlic, cumin, and coriander appear in many of the recipes and, in those from North Africa, dried fruits as well. Charcoal grilling is popular, and the Arabic word for lamb or mutton—kebab— has given its name to this style of cooking.

Generally speaking, except on feast days, meat plays a moderate role in most meals rather than a major one. Because meat is not readily available in large quantities, it is always cooked with loving care and an effort is made to bring the best out of whatever cut the cook can afford. Chicken is readily available, and the Arab cook has applied his/her ingenuity to its preparation in a variety of exciting ways. Spiced with lemon juice, grilled with olives, honey roasted, or stuffed with yellow rice and nuts are some of the recipes given.

There are other meat and chicken recipes scattered through the book, particularly in the chapter on grains and beans, where the preparation of couscous and *kibbi*, two well-known Arabic meat dishes, are described.

LAMB AND BEEF DISHES

LAMB AND APRICOT TAGINE
MOROCCO

Serves 4

This Moroccan stew combines fruit and lamb to give a delicious blend of flavors. The apricots may be replaced by prunes soaked overnight or by fresh dates, apple slices, or pear slices. The dish is traditionally served hot with cayenne, and I have left the quantity to be added to your own judgment. Serve with rice or couscous and bread.

4 tablespoons butter	*salt and black pepper*
2 pounds lamb, cut into 2-inch cubes	*cayenne (¼–½ teaspoon for mild sea-*
2 cloves garlic, put through a garlic	*soning, ¾–1 teaspoon for hot)*
press	*2 medium onions, finely sliced*
½ teaspoon turmeric or saffron	*1 cup dried whole apricots, soaked over-*
½ teaspoon ground coriander	*night*
½ teaspoon ground cumin	*juice of 1 lemon*
¼ teaspoon ground ginger	

Melt the butter in a heavy saucepan and add the meat. Cook, stirring, over moderate heat until the meat is browned on all sides. Stir in the garlic and spices, and season to taste with salt, pepper, and cayenne. Cook a further 5 minutes and add half the onion, the water the apricots were soaked in (but not the apricots), and enough further water to cover the meat. Bring to the boil, reduce the heat, cover, and simmer for 1½ hours or until the meat is tender. After 45 minutes add the remaining onion. Add more water as needed, but the sauce at the end of the cooking period should be thick. When the meat is tender add the apricots or other fruit and continue cooking until the fruit is soft but not disintegrating. Adjust the seasoning if necessary.

VARIATIONS: The lamb may be replaced by chicken parts, or a combination of both may be used.

Sometimes the meat for a *tagine* is not fried and the stewing time is increased. This method seems to give a richer flavor to the sauce and is worth trying. Follow the recipe as above, but do not fry the meat (the butter is thus not needed) and simmer the *tagine* for 2 hours. Add the apricots or other fruit after 1½ hours.

TUNISIAN LAMB TAGINE

Serves 4

The Tunisian *tagine* is prepared in the same manner as a stew, but it is then baked with cheese and eggs to give a firm pielike dish that can be cut into wedges.

4 tablespoons butter or olive oil	*¼ teaspoon nutmeg*
1 pound lamb cut into 1-inch cubes	*salt and black pepper*
2 medium onions, sliced	*6 eggs, lightly beaten*
¼ teaspoon ground ginger	*1 cup grated cheese*
½ teaspoon ground turmeric	*2 teaspoons dried mint*
½ teaspoon ground cinnamon	

Melt the butter or oil in a heavy, shallow casserole and add the lamb and onion. Stir and brown the lamb on all sides. Add the spices, salt, and pepper, stir them into the meat, and cook for a further 5 minutes. Add water to cover, bring to the boil, reduce the heat, cover, and simmer for 1 hour or until the meat is tender. Pour off the cooking liquid into a pan and reduce it to ¼–½ cups. Preheat the oven to 350° F. Cool the liquid and then combine it with the eggs, cheese, and mint. Pour this mixture over the meat in the casserole dish and sprinkle to taste with salt and pepper. Bake in the preheated oven for 20 minutes or until well set and lightly browned on top. Serve hot cut into wedges.

KOFTA (MEATBALL) AND VEGETABLE TAGINE
MOROCCO

Serves 4 to 5

The vegetables suggested may be replaced by others more available or more to your taste, such as eggplant, carrots, okra, red or green bell peppers, or green beans.

1 pound lean lamb or beef, finely ground

1 small onion, finely minced

2 tablespoons finely chopped parsley

1 tablespoon finely chopped fresh mint or 1 teaspoon dried mint

1/4 teaspoon cayenne

1/2 teaspoon ground cinnamon

1/2 teaspoon ground cumin

salt and black pepper

4 tablespoons butter

2 medium zucchini, thickly sliced

2 medium potatoes, peeled and cut into large cubes

1 1/4 cups cooked chick-peas or other beans

2 large tomatoes, skinned and quartered

4 eggs (optional)

Combine the meat, onion, parsley, mint, spices, salt, and pepper in a blender or food processor and mix to a smooth paste, or do it by hand with the back of a wooden spoon. Form the mixture into 1-inch-diameter balls. Melt the butter in a large heavy frying pan and sauté the meatballs until they are nicely browned all over. Add the vegetables and enough water to just cover. Season to taste with salt and pepper and bring to the boil. Reduce the heat, cover, and simmer until the meatballs and vegetables are tender and the liquid reduced to a good thickness. Remove the pan lid to thicken the sauce if necessary. The *tagine* may now be served.

VARIATION: Alternatively, as a variation, break the eggs carefully and separately over the top of the meatballs and vegetables and cook gently until they are set. Serve.

GROUND MEAT WITH OKRA
(Bamia)
IRAQ AND EGYPT

Serves 4 to 5

Okra is a common vegetable in the Middle East. It is usually cooked with lamb and tomato, a combination of flavors that works very well. In this recipe the meat and okra are cooked separately, then combined and baked in a dish. Serve it with a bowl of hot rice.

5 tablespoons butter

2 medium onions, finely chopped

2 cloves garlic, put through a garlic press

1/2 pounds lamb or beef, ground

1 teaspoon dried mint

3 tablespoons tomato purée

salt and black pepper to taste

1 pound okra, fresh or frozen

juice of 1 lemon

lemon wedges

Melt half the butter in a heavy pan and add the onions, garlic, and coriander. Cook over a moderate heat, stirring, until the onions are softened. Add the meat and stir and cook until it is nicely browned. Add the mint, 1 cup water, tomato purée, salt, and pepper. Mix well and, leaving the pan uncovered, gently simmer until all the liquid is absorbed. Preheat the oven to 350° F.

Wash the okra if you are using the fresh kind and you may also need to gently scrape the fuzz off the skin with a sharp knife if the okra is not young. Trim the stem ends. Melt the remaining butter in a heavy frying pan, add the okra, and sauté for 5 minutes, with frequent stirring. Put the meat mixture into a greased casserole dish and arrange the okra on top in spokelike fashion. Squeeze the lemon juice over them. Cover and bake for 40 minutes. Check during baking that the *bamia* is not drying out. Add more water or stock if needed. Serve garnished with lemon wedges.

VARIATION: This dish can be prepared with cubes of stewing beef or lamb or with pieces of chicken. If doing so the meat or chicken needs to be cooked until almost tender before being transferred to the casserole dish before the addition of the okra. To do this follow the recipe above but double the amount of water. After it has been added to the meat in the pan, cover and simmer for 1 hour or until the meat is nearly tender. Then proceed as directed in the recipe.

MEAT CROQUETTES
(Kofta)

Serves 4

Serve these croquettes hot or cold with salad and/or bean dish. They can be prepared 3–4 hours in advance, but should not be fried until just before serving.

1 pound lamb or beef, finely ground
1 medium onion, finely chopped
2 cloves garlic, put through a garlic press
1 egg, beaten
2 tablespoons freshly chopped herbs (parsley, mint, oregano, basil,

sage, etc.) or 2 teaspoons dried herbs
¼ teaspoon cayenne pepper
salt and black pepper to taste
1 cup bread crumbs
oil for frying

Combine the meat, onion, garlic, egg, herbs, cayenne, seasoning, and half the bread crumbs and thoroughly blend together. Form the mixture into small flat croquettes. Dip them into the remaining bread crumbs and fry them in the oil until nicely browned on both sides.

EGGS IN A LAMB COAT

This is a variation of the above recipe. Prepare 6 hard boiled eggs, shell them, and brush each with egg white. Prepare the meat croquette mixture as above and shape it evenly and smoothly around each of the eggs. Roll them in bread crumbs and deep fry in hot oil for about 5 minutes. Turn the eggs during frying to ensure equal cooking.

ROASTED LAMB MOROCCAN STYLE

Serves 6

Veal may be used instead of lamb.

3–4 *pound shoulder of lamb, boned, trimmed of excess fat*	2 *teaspoons ground coriander*
1 *lemon, halved*	1 *teaspoon ground cumin*
salt and black pepper	2 *cloves garlic, put through a garlic press*
1 *teaspoon paprika*	4 *tablespoons butter, softened*

Preheat the oven to 350° F. Open the shoulder up and rub both sides with the lemon halves. Sprinkle with salt and pepper all over. Combine the paprika, coriander, cumin, garlic, and butter and mix into a paste. Rub this into the meat. Tie up the shoulder, and bake it uncovered in a shallow baking dish in the preheated oven for 1½ hours or until the meat is tender and well browned.

VARIATION: The lamb, instead of being oven roasted, can be pot roasted on top of the stove. After the shoulder has been tied up, heat 4 tablespoons of oil in a large heavy pan and brown the meat on all sides. Add the juice of 1 lemon and a cup of water. Cover the pan tightly, and gently simmer over a very low heat for 2–2½ hours or until the meat is tender. Turn the meat 2–3 times during cooking.

WHOLE ROAST LAMB
(Khouzi)
GULF STATES

Serves 15 to 20

Whole roast lamb is a very special desert feast prepared for important ceremonies and festivals. It cannot normally be prepared in a domestic kitchen, but it can be roasted on a spit over a charcoal fire or baked in a large catering oven. The recipe is interesting to wonder over even if you do not put it into practice. However, it is also possible to use the same recipe for stuffing and roasting small cuts of meat by following the same method but reducing quantities proportionately.

1 baby lamb about 20 pounds	*2 tablespoons oil*
½ cup butter, softened	*2 medium onions, finely chopped*
4 cloves garlic, put through a garlic press	*¾ cup blanched almonds*
	¾ cup walnuts, chopped
2 tablespoons ground coriander	*¾ cup pine nuts (optional)*
1 teaspoon ground paprika	*¾ cup raisins*
1 teaspoon ground ginger	*3 pounds (15 cups) cooked long-grain rice*
2 teaspoons ground cumin	
salt and black pepper	*1 small chicken, ready for stuffing*

Ask the butcher to prepare the lamb for stuffing and roasting. Wipe the lamb inside and out with a damp cloth. Combine the butter, garlic, and spices into a paste. Rub the lamb with this inside and out, and set it aside. Brown the onions in the oil and combine with the nuts and raisins. Stir this mixture into the rice and season to taste with salt and pepper. Stuff the chicken with some of the mixture. Place some rice mixture in the cavity of the lamb and then stuff the chicken in. Pack in the remaining rice mixture tightly and sew up the cavity. Preheat the oven to 350° F. Put the lamb in a large baking dish and place it in the oven. Baste it in its own juices during cooking and turn it over once or twice. Bake for about 3 hours or until it is tender and cooked to your liking. Serve on a large platter if possible, with the cavity opened up and with the chicken and some stuffing on display.

To roast on a spit, push the spit rod down the length of the lamb, securing it against the backbone. Truss the legs together and roast over glowing charcoal. The lamb should ideally be 12 inches away from the charcoal bed. Baste it often with melted butter sesoned with crushed garlic and ground coriander. When done the lamb should be crisp and brown on the outside and well cooked inside. The time needed depends on the weight of the lamb, but 3 hours for a medium lamb is a rough guide.

VARIATION: The rice stuffing and cooking methods used in this recipe may also be used with other cuts of meat such as shoulder of lamb. Reduce the quantities and cooking times accordingly.

STUFFED BREAST OF VEAL OR LAMB
FERTILE CRESCENT

Serves 8

4 pounds breast of veal or lamb	*½ teaspoon ground cardamom*
juice of 1 lemon	*¼ teaspoon ground ginger*
salt and black pepper	*½ cup almonds*
oil for frying	*¾ cup raisins*
1 medium onion, finely chopped	*1 cup water or stock*
½ pound ground lamb	*10 cups cooked rice*
½ teaspoon ground cinnamon	

Cut a pouch or pocket into the breast of meat for the stuffing (or ask the butcher to do it). Rub the meat with lemon juice and sprinkle all over with salt and pepper. Set it aside while you prepare the stuffing. Heat a little oil in a heavy frying pan and lightly brown the onion. Add the lamb, spices, half the almonds, and all the raisins. Fry and stir until the meat is browned. Add the water or stock, season to taste with salt and pepper, and simmer over a low heat until all the liquid is absorbed. Stir in the cooked rice and leave it to cool. Preheat the oven to 350° F. Stuff the breast of lamb or veal with the meat and rice mixture, rub it with a little oil, then roast it uncovered, in a shallow pan, for 1½ hours or until the meat is tender and browned. Serve garnished with the remainder of the almonds lightly fried in a little oil.

VARIATIONS: The stuffing recipe given for whole roast lamb (below) may also be used in the recipe.
    This stuffing may be used with other cuts of meat suitable for stuffing and roasting.

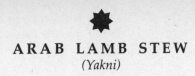

ARAB LAMB STEW
(Yakni)

Serves 4 to 6

Lamb stew is made in hundreds of different ways all over the Middle East. It is the staple main meat dish of many people and provides a nourishing and tasty meal which can utilize the seasonally changing ingredients available to the cook. The basic formula is the same: a small amount of meat is fried, one of the vegetables in season (or a mixture of them) is added, and the whole is spiced, seasoned, and simmered until the meat is tender. Uncooked but soaked beans or lentils are added at the start of the simmering period or toward the end if they are precooked. Leafy green vegetables such as spinach or cabbage are added at the end, and the dish is served with rice, salad, and plain yogurt. The recipe given here is a general one, and you can make your own selection of vegetables and beans. The most popular Arab vegetables are, eggplants, okra, and spinach.

2 tablespoons oil or *melted butter*
2 *medium onions, sliced*
3 *cloves garlic, put through a garlic press*
1 *teaspoon ground coriander*
1 *pound stewing lamb, chopped into small pieces*

Vegetables· 1 *pound selected from the following:*
eggplant cubed, salted 30 minutes, rinsed, and drained
okra, trim stem ends, scrape off fur if necessary
green beans, topped, tailed, and cut into 2-inch lengths
zucchini, sliced

spinach, washed
squash, cubed
red or green peppers, cored, de seeded, and chopped
carrots, peeled and chopped
potatoes, peeled and cubed

water or stock
3 *tablespoons tomato purée*
2 *tablespoons chopped fresh herbs (parsley, mint, coriander, etc.)*
½ *teaspoon allspice*
1 *teaspoon cinnamon*
salt and black pepper
1¼ *cups beans, dried peas, or lentils, soaked overnight, cooked until tender*

Heat the oil or butter in a heavy pan and add the onions, garlic, and coriander. Stir-fry over moderate heat until the onion is just browned. Add the mean and brown it all over. Stir in the vegetables (leave the spinach if used until later) and sauté for 5 minutes. Cover the contents of the pan with water or stock, add the tomato pureé, herbs, and spices, and season to taste with salt and pepper. Bring to the boil, reduce the heat, cover, and simmer for 1–1½ hours or until the meat is tender. Toward the end of the cooking period add the cooked beans, and spinach if used.

EGYPTIAN BEEF STEW WITH EGGS
(Dfeena)

Serves 6

In this traditional recipe the stew is cooked over a low heat for a long period. The eggs in their shells are cooked in the stew, and the process gives them a distinctive flavor. The dish can be prepared in the morning and served at night or cooked overnight and then reheated when required (unless you would like it for breakfast!).

2 tablespoons olive oil
2 medium onions, chopped
3 cloves garlic, put through a garlic press
1 pound stewing beef, cut into large pieces
1¼ cups chick-peas, soaked overnight, drained

1 pound potatoes, peeled and cut into large pieces
½ teaspoon ground ginger
1 teaspoon nutmeg
salt and black pepper
water or stock
6 eggs, washed

In a heavy pan with a tight-fitting lid heat the oil. Add the onions and garlic and lightly brown. Add the meat and brown it all over. Stir in the chick-peas and cook, stirring, for a few minutes. Add the potatoes and spices and mix well. Season to taste with salt and pepper and add water or stock to cover. Gently place the eggs in the pot so that they are covered. Bring it to the boil, reduce the heat, cover, and cook over a very low heat for 8–10 hours. Before serving, shell the eggs and return them to the pot.

LAMB WITH PRUNES
NORTH AFRICA

Serves 4

This dish is from North Africa where meat and dried fruits are a popular combination. Serve it with rice.

2 tablespoons butter or olive oil
1½ pounds lamb, cubed
1 medium onion, sliced
3 cloves garlic, put through a garlic press
½ teaspoon turmeric or saffron
1 cinnamon stick broken into 1-inch lengths or 1 teaspoon ground cinnamon

salt and black pepper to taste
1 tablespoon flour
water or stock
1½ cups prunes, soaked in water and pitted

Heat the butter or oil in a heavy pan and brown the lamb cubes all over. Remove the lamb to a plate and set aside. Fry the onion and garlic in the same pan in the juices and fat left by the meat until lightly browned. Add the turmeric or saffron, cinnamon, and seasoning, stir well, and sauté for a few minutes. Stir in the flour and cook a little longer. Slowly mix in 2½ cups water or stock, return the meat to the pan, bring to the boil, reduce the heat, and adjust the seasoning. Cover and simmer for 1 hour or until the lamb is nearly tender. Add the prunes, cover, and simmer for a further 10 minutes.

VARIATION: Add 1 cup chopped walnuts or whole blanched almonds or pine nuts to the ingredients at the same time as the spices. Substitute dried apricots or raisins for the prunes.

LAMB WITH DATES
IRAQ

Proceed as in the above recipe, but replace the prunes with dates prepared as follows: put 1 cup chopped dates in a small pan with a cup of water. Cook until the dates are very soft and then purée in a blender or press through a sieve. Add this purée in place of the prunes.

LAMB WITH CUMIN
EGYPT

Serves 4

This is a very simple but flavorsome dish. Serve with rice, salad, pickles, pita bread, and a bowl of plain yogurt.

4 tablespoons butter
1½ pounds lamb, cubed
6 cloves garlic, put through a garlic press

1 teaspoon ground cumin
1 teaspoon cumin seeds
water or stock
salt and black pepper

In a heavy pan melt the butter and brown the meat on all sides. Add the garlic, cumin, and cumin seeds and stir and cook for 5 minutes. Just cover with water or stock, season to taste with salt and pepper, and bring to the boil. Reduce heat, cover, and simmer for 1 hour or until the meat is tender.

BAKED LAMB AND VEGETABLES
EGYPT

Serves 4 to 6

¼ pound butter
½ small cauliflower, separated into florets
2 medium eggplants, thickly sliced, salted 30 minutes, and drained
2 medium green or red peppers, cored, deseeded, and chopped
2 medium tomatoes, peeled and chopped
1 teaspoon allspice

salt and black pepper
1 medium onion, sliced
1 pound lamb, ground
1 teaspoon ground coriander
1 teaspoon paprika
1 teaspoon dried thyme
1 teaspoon dried sage
1 cup grated cheese (Swiss, Cheddar, Gruyère, or Monterey Jack)

Melt half the butter in a heavy pan and add the vegetables (except the onion) in the order given, cooking each a little before adding the next. Finally, sauté with continual stirring until they are all softened. Stir in the allspice, salt, and pepper, then remove the vegetables from the pan to a large dish. Melt the remaining butter in the same pan, add the onion, and lightly brown. Stir in the lamb, spices, and herbs, and brown the meat. Season to taste with salt and pepper. Break up any lumps that may form. Preheat the oven to 400° F. Grease a casserole dish and layer the meat and vegetables in it. Finish with a layer of vegetables. Sprinkle the cheese over the top and bake in the oven for 30 minutes or until the cheese is browned and bubbly.

BAKED LAMB AND EGGPLANT

Serves 4

1 large eggplant, thickly sliced, salted 30 minutes, drained	1 teaspoon cinnamon
½ cup olive oil	¼ teaspoon cayenne
2 medium onions, sliced	salt and black pepper to taste
1 pound lamb, ground	2 tablespoons butter
	5 cups cooked long-grain rice

Pat the eggplant dry. Heat half the oil in a heavy frying pan and brown the eggplant slices on both sides. Remove them from the pan and set them aside. Add the remaining oil to the pan and sauté the onions until golden. Add the meat, spices, and seasoning and cook, stirring, until the meat is browned. Break up any lumps that form. Preheat the oven to 350° F. Butter a casserole dish, cover the bottom with one-third of the rice, add a layer of half the eggplant slices, then add half the meat mixture. Repeat, ending with a top layer of rice. Cover and bake for 45 minutes. Remove the cover for the last 10 minutes of the cooking time.

VARIATION: Sprinkle grated cheese over the top of the last layer of rice and serve with the cheese browned and bubbling.

MEAT AND WHEAT STEW
(Harissa)
FERTILE CRESCENT

Serves 4

This very simple peasant dish is delicious on a cold day.

1 pound stewing lamb or beef, cubed	salt and black pepper
2 pints water	2 tablespoons butter
2½ cups whole wheat, soaked over-	1 teaspoon ground cumin
night, drained	1 teaspoon ground cinnamon

Put the meat and 5 cups water in a heavy saucepan and bring to the boil. Remove any scum that forms and add the wheat. Season to taste with salt and pepper, cover the pan, and simmer slowly for 2½–3 hours or until the meat is falling apart and the wheat is very soft. Beat the contents of the pan with a wooden spoon or whisk to form a coarse purée of meat and wheat. Melt the butter in a small frying pan, add the cumin and cinnamon, and cook until the butter browns. Serve the stew in bowls with the spiced butter poured over.

MARINATED LAMB KEBABS
NORTH AFRICA

Serves 6

This is a basic kebab recipe. You may add more vegetables to it, or different types of meat may be substituted. It is also suitable for fish or poultry. Serve with chopped onion and cucumber, shredded lettuce, and pita bread.

4 tablespoons olive oil	½ teaspoon ground cumin
juice of 2 lemons	½ teaspoon turmeric
2 cloves garlic put through a garlic	2 tablespoons chopped parsley
press	2 pounds boned lamb (leg is good), cut
2 teaspoons salt	into 1-inch cubes
1 teaspoon freshly ground black pepper	1 large onion, quartered and divided
½ teaspoon ground ginger	into separate leaves

Put the first nine ingredients in a mixing bowl and stir until well mixed. Add the meat and onion and stir until they are evenly coated in the marinade. Cover and set aside for 2–6 hours. Thread the meat and onions onto skewers and cook over glowing charcoal or under a broiler until the meat is tender. Turn during cooking and baste liberally with marinade. Slide the kebabs off the skewers directly onto serving plates.

LAMB WITH LEMON JUICE
MOROCCO

Serves 4

This Moroccan dish is cooked in the traditional manner, in which the meat is rubbed with oil and spices and then simmered in water until cooked. The cooking stock is then reduced and served as a sauce. Serve with rice and salad.

4 tablespoons olive oil
2 cloves garlic, put through a garlic press
½ teaspoon ground saffron or turmeric
1 teaspoon ground coriander
pinch of ginger

1½ pounds lean lamb, cubed
1 medium onion, chopped
2 lemons, quartered
salt and black pepper
½ cup olives (optional)

Combine the oil, garlic, saffron or turmeric, coriander, and ginger and stir the lamb in the mixture until each piece is coated. Transfer the whole to a heavy pan and just cover with water. Add the onion and lemon, season to taste with salt and pepper, and bring to the boil. Reduce the heat, cover, and simmer for 1 hour or until the lamb is tender. Remove the lamb to a plate with a perforated spoon. Reduce the sauce to a thickness of your liking. In the meanwhile cover the olives (if used) in cold water in a small pan and bring to the boil. Drain and repeat the process. Put the lamb and treated olives back in the reduced sauce and heat through, stirring. Adjust the seasoning.

LAMB WITH RICE AND EGGPLANT
IRAQ

Serves 4

Another colorful and tasty dish with layers of red rice, creamy eggplant and golden-brown pieces of lamb.

1 large eggplant, thinly sliced	1 teaspoon cinnamon
salt	1 teaspoon allspice
½ cup butter or olive oil	salt and black pepper
2 cloves garlic, put through a garlic press	1 cup long-grain rice (brown or white)
1 medium onion, diced	½ tomato purée
4 lamb cutlets (total weight 1–2 pounds)	2½ boiling water or stock

Place the eggplant slices in a colander, sprinkle generously with salt, and leave for 30–60 minutes. Rinse and pat dry. Heat half the butter or oil in a heavy frying pan, sauté the garlic until soft, add the onion, and sauté until golden. Place the lamb cutlets in the pan and brown on both sides. Arrange the onion and cutlets in the base of a 4-pint heavy casserole. Preheat the oven to 350° F. Heat the remaining butter or oil in the frying pan and gently brown the eggplant slices on both sides. Layer the eggplant slices over the cutlets, and sprinkle the cinnamon and allspice over them. Season to taste with salt and pepper. Spread the rice over the top. Combine the tomato purée with the water or stock and pour into the casserole. Cover and bake for 1 hour or until the rice is tender. Place a large serving dish over the top of the casserole and invert the contents onto the dish.

VARIATION: Replace the lamb cutlets with 1½ pounds cubed lamb or beef.

RICE WITH LAMB CASSEROLE
(Roz Tajin)
FERTILE CRESCENT

Serves 6

Serve this with plain yogurt or yogurt and cucumber.

1½ pounds lean lamb, diced	2 tablespoons tomato purée
2 medium onions, quartered	salt and black pepper
½ cup butter or olive oil	2 cups long-grain rice, washed and drained
1 teaspoon cinnamon	2½ cups boiling water
4 tablespoons pine nuts or chopped almonds	

Preheat the oven to 350° F. Sauté the lamb and onions in the butter or oil in a heavy frying pan over low heat until the meat is almost tender. Stir in the cinnamon and nuts and sauté until the nuts are lightly browned. Stir in the tomato purée, season to taste with salt and pepper, and transfer the mixture to the bottom of a heavy casserole. Distribute it evenly and spread the rice over the top. Pour in the boiling water. Cover and transfer to the preheated oven. Bake for 1 hour or until the rice is tender. Place a large serving dish over the top of the casserole and invert the contents onto the dish.

VARIATION: Add 1 tablespoon fresh chopped mint or 1 teaspoon dried mint to the pan with the tomato purée. Fifteen minutes before the end of the baking period sprinkle grated cheese over the contents of the casserole and continue baking.

LAMB WITH BEANS AND RICE
SYRIA

Serves 4

This dish looks very appetizing when served with its colorful layers of rice, beans, and meat.

2 tablespoons olive oil
2 cloves garlic, put through a garlic press
1 medium onion, sliced
1 pound lean lamb, cut into 1-inch cubes
1 teaspoon allspice
1 teaspoon ground coriander
2 cups boiling water
1 cup cooked beans (e.g., haricot, chick-peas, etc.)
1 cup long-grain rice, washed and drained
salt and black pepper

Heat the oil in a heavy pot and lightly brown the garlic and onion. Add the lamb and sauté over low heat until the lamb is browned on all sides. Stir in the spices and boiling water and simmer, covered, for 20 minutes. Add the beans and rice, seasoned to taste with salt and pepper, and return the pot to the boil. Reduce the heat, cover, and simmer for 20 minutes or until the rice and meat are tender. Add a little more water if the pot dries up during the cooking time, although ideally all liquid should have been absorbed by the end of the cooking period. Invert the pot over a serving dish. Remove the pot, leaving a mound of rice topped with beans and lamb.

YEMENI BEEF AND RICE

Serves 4

yellow rice cooked by Method I or II
  (page 130)
4 tablespoons sesame seed oil
1 medium onion, finely chopped
12 ounces ground beef

1 teaspoon curry powder
salt and black pepper
1 tablespoon chopped mint or 1 teaspoon dried mint
2 hard-boiled eggs, peeled and sliced

Put the rice on to cook, using Method I or II (see pp. 130–131). Heat the oil in a heavy frying pan, add the onion, and sauté until just soft. Stir in the meat and curry powder and cook, stirring, until the meat is cooked through. Season to taste with salt and pepper and stir in the mint. Gently stir this mixture into the rice in the pot in which it was cooked. Cover the pot with a tight-fitting lid and place it over low heat for 5 minutes. Remove from the heat and serve topped with slices of hard-boiled egg.

VARIATION: If you can obtain them, substitute the curry powder with ½ cup fenugreek seeds, soaked overnight, drained, and crushed.

SKEWERED LIVER WITH GARLIC
LEBANON

Serves 4

1 pound lamb or calf liver
4 cloves garlic, put through a garlic
  press
1 teaspoon dried mint

¼ cup oil (olive oil is best)
salt and black pepper to taste
lemon wedges

Wash the liver and remove the skin. Slice into ½-inch strips and cut the strips into 1-inch squares. Combine the garlic and mint in a bowl, put the liver pieces in, and evenly coat them with the mixture. Pour in the oil and sprinkle with salt and pepper. Stir the liver about to evenly coat it. Set aside for 30 minutes. Thread the liver on skewers and cook over a glowing charcoal fire or under a broiler. Turn during cooking and brush with the residue of the oil and garlic mixture from the bowl. Serve when lightly browned on both sides. Push the liver pieces from the skewer onto serving plates and provide lemon wedges for squeezing juice liberally on to the kebabs.

VARIATION: Alternate pieces of onion and/or red/green pepper and/or cubes of eggplant with the liver on the skewers.

LIVER AND KIDNEY CASSEROLE
YEMEN

Serves 4 to 6

Serve this with a fresh green salad and rice.

1 pound lamb or calf kidneys	*1 teaspoon turmeric*
1 pound lamb or calf livers	*½ teaspoon ground cumin*
4 tablespoons butter	*1 teaspoon ground coriander*
1 medium onion, sliced	*2 medium tomatoes, peeled and chopped*
4 cloves garlic, put through a garlic press	*salt and black pepper*

Wash the kidneys, remove the outer skins, and cut out any fatty cores. Dry on paper towels and cut into 1-inch cubes. Wash the liver, drain, remove the fine skin, and cut into 1-inch cubes. Dry on paper towels. Heat the butter in a heavy saucepan, add the onion and garlic, and lightly brown them. Stir in the turmeric, cumin, and coriander and add the livers and kidneys. Fry over a high heat until the meat is browned all over. Add the tomatoes, water to cover, and salt and pepper to taste. Bring to the boil, reduce the heat, cover, and simmer for 1 hour or until the meat is tender. The sauce can be reduced if it is too thin by leaving the pan uncovered during the last 5–10 minutes of cooking.

CHICKEN DISHES

HOT SPICED CHICKEN
WITH LEMON JUICE
NORTH AFRICA

Serves 5 to 6

The chicken is rubbed with spicy garlic mixture and then fried before casseroling in water, spices, and tomato purée. Finally the dish is given its distinctive taste by the addition of lemon juice. Serve with rice and/ or pita bread and pickles or see the variation below.

1 chicken, about 3 pounds	2 medium onions, finely chopped
1 tablespoon salt	4 cloves
3 cloves garlic, put through a garlic press	2 teaspoons cumin seeds
	1 teaspoon coriander seeds
½ teaspoon cayenne pepper	2 tablespoons tomato purée
1 teaspoon turmeric	juice of 2 lemons
¼ cup olive oil or melted butter	

Cut the chicken into serving pieces, and wipe the pieces dry. Combine the salt, garlic, cayenne, and turmeric and rub the mixture into the skin side of the chicken pieces. Leave for 15 minutes. Heat the oil or melted butter in a large heavy frying pan and brown the chicken on both sides. Remove the pieces to a plate and in the same oil lightly fry the chopped onion until just soft. Stir in the cloves, cumin, and coriander seeds and continue frying. After a few minutes stir in the tomato purée and put in the chicken pieces. Add ¾ cup water, cover the pan tightly, and simmer gently for 1 hour or until the chicken is tender. After 45 minutes' cooking time add the lemon juice and adjust the seasoning to taste.

VARIATION: This dish is excellent cooked with rice, and the procedure requires little adjustment to the recipe. Wash and drain 1½ cups long-grain rice. Add it to the chicken after 35–40 minutes cooking time and also pour in 1½ cups boiling water. Cover the pan tightly and simmer gently until rice and chicken are both tender. Lightly stir once during cooking. Transfer the contents of the pan to one large serving dish, arrange the chicken pieces on top of the rice, and serve.

YELLOW CHICKEN WITH ALMONDS
EGYPT

Serves 4 to 6

1 chicken, about 3 pounds
salt and freshly ground black pepper to
  taste
½ cups olive oil or melted butter
4 cloves garlic, put through a garlic
  press

½ teaspoon turmeric or saffron
2 tablespoons finely chopped parsley
1¼ cups boiling water or chicken stock
½ cup whole almonds, blanched
4 hard-boiled eggs, shelled and sliced

Cut the chicken into serving pieces and lightly sprinkle them with salt
and pepper. Heat three-quarters of the oil or butter in a heavy frying
pan and lightly sauté the garlic, add the turmeric or saffron, and stir it
into the hot oil and garlic. Add the chicken and brown it on both sides.
Sprinkle in the parsley and pour in the boiling water or stock. Cover the
pan tightly and simmer gently for 1 hour or until the chicken is tender.
Turn the chicken pieces 2–3 times during cooking, and toward the end
of the cooking time adjust the seasoning to taste. Add more water or
stock if the pan dries out. Just before the chicken is ready brown the
almonds in the remaining oil and drain them on absorbent paper. Serve
the chicken smothered in almonds and garnished with slices of hard-
boiled egg.

VARIATION: Sometimes the almonds are cooked along with the chicken
to give a stronger almond flavor to the sauce. If you would like to try
this method, sauté the almonds with the garlic at the beginning of the
recipe and then proceed as directed.

GRILLED CHICKEN
(Farareej Mashwi)
EGYPT

Serves 4 to 6

This recipe uses very few ingredients to produce chicken pieces as tasty
as you have ever had! The method can also be used for pigeon, quail,
duck, or pheasant.

2 small or spring boiler chickens, quartered
salt and black pepper

4 cloves garlic, put through a garlic
press
6 tablespoons olive oil
juice of 2 lemons

Season the chicken pieces with salt and pepper. Combine the garlic, oil, and lemon juice in a shallow dish, add the chicken pieces, and brush them all over with this mixture. Leave to marinate for 1 hour.

To cook under a broiler, preheat and oil the rack. Drain the chicken pieces and place them skin side down on the rack. Set the rack with a pan below it under the heat so that the chicken pieces are at least 6 inches away from the heat source. Grill until the side facing the heat source is nicely browned, brushing occasionally with the marinade. Turn the chicken pieces over and repeat for the other side. Serve when the pieces are golden brown and crisp. Pour over them any cooking juices and remaining marinade.

To cook over charcoal, put the chicken pieces skin side up on a well-oiled rack and cook over a glowing charcoal fire. Brush often with the marinade and turn the pieces 2–3 times during cooking. Serve when brown and crisp but still moist on the inside.

CHICKEN WITH CHICK-PEAS
MOROCCO

Serves 6

In this dish the chicken is left whole during cooking and all the vital juices stay in the pot.

1 roasting chicken, about 3 pounds
½ cup butter or olive oil
3 medium onions, finely chopped
¼ teaspoon cayenne
1 teaspoon turmeric
4 cloves garlic, put through a garlic
press

juice of 2 lemons
1¼ cups chick-peas, soaked overnight
and drained
salt and black pepper
2 tablespoons finely chopped parsley
2 tablespoons raisins (optional)

Clean the chicken inside and out with a damp cloth. Heat the butter or oil in a large deep flameproof casserole dish or saucepan (big enough to hold a whole chicken) and stir in one-third of the onions and all of the cayenne and turmeric. Gently fry them, add the chicken, and fry it, turning, until it is nicely yellowed all over. Add the garlic, lemon juice, chick-peas, and enough water to just cover the chicken. Season to taste with salt and pepper. Bring to the boil, cover, and simmer for 1 hour or until the chicken is tender. During the last half hour of cooking add the remaining onions, the parsley, and the raisins. Toward the end of the cooking period, adjust the seasoning, and if the cooking liquid is too thin, leave the lid off the pan to reduce it. Serve with the chicken cut into pieces and the chick-pea sauce poured over the top.

CHICKEN WITH OLIVES
MOROCCO

Serves 4

Chicken, olives, and spices with lemon juice provide an unusual and refreshing combination of flavors. Serve with couscous or rice and lemon wedges.

1 cup black or green olives, or a mixture	1 small onion, finely sliced
	1 teaspoon ground ginger
1 chicken, about 3 pounds, cut into serving pieces	½ teaspoon turmeric
	salt and black pepper to taste
½ cup olive oil	juice of 2 lemons
2 cloves garlic, put through a garlic press	

Cover the olives with water, bring to the boil, drain, repeat, and set aside (this reduces their bitterness). In a heavy frying pan or casserole dish fry the chicken pieces in the oil until lightly browned on both sides. Add the garlic, onion, ginger, turmeric, salt, and pepper, and continue frying for a further 5 minutes. Turn and move the chicken about during this time. Add 2 cups of boiling water and cover the pan or dish tightly. Simmer gently until the chicken is nearly tender (when a skewer pushed into the chicken meets a little resistance and draws a slightly pink juice). Remove the lid, add the olives and lemon juice, and continue cooking uncovered until the chicken is tender (when the skewer meets very little resistance and the juice is clear) and the sauce is quite thick.

HONEY ROASTED CHICKEN
LEBANON

Serves 4

This method produces a sweet golden-brown chicken complemented by a garnish of chopped ginger and almonds. To reduce cooking time cut up the chicken before roasting.

1 roasting chicken, about 3–4 pounds, cleaned and wiped dry	4 tablespoons honey
1 lemon	chopped preserved ginger or grated fresh ginger (optional)
salt	chopped almonds, (optional)
4 tablespoons butter	

Preheat the oven to 450° F. Cut the lemon in half and rub the chicken inside and out with one half. Sprinkle the chicken inside and out with salt. Melt the butter and whisk it into the honey together with the juice of the remaining half lemon. Brush the chicken inside and out with this mixture. Place the chicken in a well-oiled roasting pan and place in the oven. Reduce the heat after 10 minutes to 350° F and cook for about 20 minutes per pound of bird. Baste occasionally during cooking. Serve the chicken cut up and garnished with preserved ginger and chopped almonds.

CURRIED ROASTED CHICKEN
GULF STATES

Serves 4

This is nothing like the ubiquitous (but sometimes delicious) chicken curry sold in Indian restaurants. The curry powder is made into a paste and rubbed into the chicken before roasting, imparting a mild flavor that permeates the whole chicken. To reduce cooking time the chicken can be cut up before roasting.

1 roasting chicken, about 3–4 pounds,
  cleaned and wiped dry
salt
½ cup butter, melted
juice of 1 lemon
1 teaspoon thyme

1 teaspoon curry powder
¼ teaspoon cayenne
½ teaspoon cinnamon
¼ teaspoon nutmeg
salt and pepper

Preheat the oven to 450° F. Sprinkle the outside and inside of the chicken with salt. Combine the remaining ingredients, using only half the butter, and mix into a smooth paste. Rub this into the chicken inside and out. Put the remaining butter in a roasting pan and place in the oven for a few minutes. Now put the chicken in the pan and return it to the oven. Reduce the heat after 10 minutes to 350° F and cook for about 20 minutes per 1 pound of chicken or until tender. During cooking baste occasionally with the pan juices.

VARIATION: For golden-brown chicken follow the recipe above but substitute ½ teaspoon saffron powder and 1 teaspoon turmeric for the curry powder, cayenne, and nutmeg.

ROAST CHICKEN STUFFED WITH RICE
(Dajaj Mahshi)
SYRIA

Serves 6

The stuffing can be made 3–4 hours before it is needed.

1 large roasting chicken, about 4
  pounds, or 2 small roasting chickens,
  about 2 pounds each
salt and black pepper
½ cup butter
1 large onion, finely chopped
liver and heart of the chicken, finely
  chopped

4 tablespoons pine nuts (optional)
1 cup rice, washed and drained
2 cups water or chicken stock
4 tablespoons raisins, washed
2 tablespoons finely chopped parsley or
  coriander

Pat the chicken dry inside and out with paper towels and season all over with salt and pepper. Set aside in a cool place. Melt half the butter in a heavy frying pan and add the onion. Sauté over medium heat until just soft. Add the liver, heart, and pine nuts and continue frying, while stirring, until the meat is sealed all over. Stir in the rice and stir-fry for a further few minutes. Add the water or stock, raisins, and parsley or coriander. Season to taste with salt and pepper, bring to the boil, reduce the heat, cover, and simmer for 20 minutes or until the rice has absorbed all the liquid. Meanwhile preheat the oven to 450° F. Stuff the chicken with the mixture. Reserve any stuffing left over and serve it warmed up with the chicken. Secure the chicken opening with skewers. Melt the remaining butter in a baking dish, put the chicken in the dish breast side up, and brush with the butter. Bake in the preheated oven. After 10 minutes reduce the heat to 350° F and bake for about 20 minutes per pound of chicken. During cooking occasionally baste the chicken with the pan juices.

VARIATION: Replace the rice with 1 cup of coarse bulghul wheat, pre-soaked and drained. Reduce the water or stock used to 1 cup and reduce the simmering time for the stuffing mixture from 20 minutes to 5 minutes. Otherwise follow the same procedure.

SPICY STUFFED CHICKEN
MOROCCAN STYLE

Serves 6

In this method the whole chicken is browned in butter, stuffed, and then simmered (not roasted) over a low heat until cooked. The stuffing can be made 3–4 hours before it is needed.

1 *3–4-pound roasting chicken, or 2 Cornish hens, about 2 pounds each*
salt and black pepper
½ *cup butter*
1 *small onion, finely chopped*
1 *cup rice, washed and drained*
4 *tablespoons chopped walnuts or almonds*

4 *tablespoons raisins, washed and drained*
½ *teaspoon ground ginger*
½ *teaspoon cayenne*
1 *teaspoon cinnamon*
½ *teaspoon nutmeg*
½ *teaspoon turmeric or saffron*
2 *cups water or chicken stock*

Pat the chickens dry with paper towels and season all over with salt and pepper. Set aside in a cool place. Melt half the butter in a heavy frying pan and sauté the onion until it is just softened. Stir in the rice, walnuts, or almonds, and raisins and stir-fry over a moderate heat for 2–3 minutes. Combine the spices and add half the mixture together with half the water to the frying pan, season to taste with salt and pepper, and mix well. Bring to the boil, cover, reduce heat, and simmer until all the liquid is absorbed. Meanwhile in a heavy casserole dish melt the remaining butter and brown the whole chickens all over. Allow the rice mixture and chickens to cool a little and then stuff the chickens and secure the openings with skewers. Reserve any stuffing left over and serve it warmed up with the chicken. Put the stuffing left over and serve it warmed up with the chicken. Put the chickens into the casserole dish. Combine the remaining water and spices and bring to the boil. Add the mixture to the dish, cover, and simmer over a low heat for 1½ hours or until the chickens are tender. Add more water as needed.

VARIATION: Remove the chickens from the dish just before they are tender. Drain and them brush them with oil and bake in a preheated oven at 400° F for 15 minutes or until browned and tender.

MEAT-STUFFED CHICKEN
LEBANON

Prepare the following stuffing and then follow one of the procedures described in the previous two recipes for stuffing and cooking the chicken. If desired, the stuffing can be made 3–4 hours in advance.

3 tablespoons olive oil	½ teaspoon cinnamon
1 pound beef or lamb, ground	¼ teaspoon nutmeg
1 cup chopped walnuts or almonds	salt and black pepper to taste
½ cup pine nuts	3 cups slightly undercooked rice

Heat the oil in a frying pan over medium heat and fry the meat, while stirring, until browned. Add the nuts, spices, and seasoning, mix well, and fry a further few minutes. Remove from the heat and stir in the rice. Adjust the seasoning and the stuffing is ready.

FRIED CHICKEN WITH SPINACH
EGYPT

Serves 5 to 6

This dish is traditionally made with *melokhia*, a green leafy vegetable popular in Egypt, but spinach works well in the recipe.

1 chicken, about 3½ pounds, cut in pieces	4 cloves garlic, put through a garlic press
1 medium onion, halved	½ cup butter
1 carrot	1 pound spinach, washed, drained, and chopped
salt and black pepper to taste	
1 teaspoon ground coriander	

Put the chicken pieces, onion, and carrot in a large pan, just cover with water, season with salt and pepper, and bring to the boil. Cover, reduce the heat, and simmer until the chicken is tender. Remove the chicken, drain, and reserve the stock. Combine the coriander, garlic, and 2 teaspoons salt and crush them into a paste. Clean the pan and melt the butter in it over a moderate heat. Stir in the paste and then add the chicken. Sauté the pieces, turning, until they are colored all over. Add the spinach and cook until it is wilted and tender. Adjust the seasoning, and serve with rice and the hot stock in separate bowls.

CHICKEN TAGINE
MOROCCO

Serves 5 to 6

Tagine is a Moroccan dish in which pieces of chicken or lamb are gently simmered in water and spices until tender. The cooking stock is then reduced and served as a sauce over the meat.

1 chicken, about 3½ pounds, cut in pieces	4 tablespoons butter
2 cloves garlic, put through a garlic press	2 medium onions, sliced
	1 cup chick-peas or other dried beans, soaked overnight, drained
½ teaspoon turmeric	½ teaspoon paprika
¼ teaspoon ground ginger	½ cup olives (optional)
2 tablespoons olive oil	2 tablespoons chopped parsley
salt and black pepper	juice of 1 lemon

Pat the chicken pieces dry with paper towels. Combine the garlic, turmeric, ginger, and oil and rub the mixture into the chicken. Season the pieces with salt and pepper and set aside for 1 hour. Put the chicken, the butter, and half the onion in a large pan and just cover with water. Bring to the boil, add the chick-peas and paprika, adjust the seasoning, cover, and simmer for 1–1½ hours or until the chick-peas and chicken are almost tender. Add more water if needed. Meanwhile cover the olives with cold water in a saucepan and bring to the boil, drain, and repeat the process. Add the olives, remaining onion, and parsley to the pan and continue cooking. When the chicken is tender remove it from the pan to a hot plate and keep warm in the oven. Reduce the sauce to a moderate thickness. Serve the chicken with lemon juice squeezed over and then the sauce poured over.

VARIATION: Substitute ½ cup of chopped nuts for the olives and add with the second batch of onion.

CHICKEN, RICE, AND ORANGE PILAV
MOROCCO

Serves 4 to 6

This dish takes simple ingredients and turns them into an exotic feast of subtle flavors.

2–3-pound boiling chicken, cut into 6 pieces	shredded peel of 1 orange
salt to taste	1 teaspoon ground cardamom
2 medium onions, thinly sliced	1 teaspoon ground cinnamon
1 cup thinly sliced carrots	½ teaspoon turmeric or saffron
4 tablespoons butter or oil	1 cup long-grain rice
	salt and black pepper

Put the chicken pieces in a saucepan, add 3 cups water and salt, and bring to the boil. Skim off any foam that forms, reduce the heat, cover the pot, and simmer until the chicken pieces are almost tender but not to the point where the meat is falling off the bone. Remove the chicken from the pan and cut off the lean meat. Discard the fat, skin, and bones. Reserve the stock in the pan. In a large frying pan sauté the onions and carrots in the butter or oil until the onions start to brown. Stir in the orange peel, spices, and rice and season with salt and pepper. Stir and fry for 2 minutes. Put the chicken pieces in the bottom of the saucepan, cover with the contents of the frying pan, and spread the mixture evenly. Bring 2 cups of the reserved chicken stock to the boil and pour it into the pan. Cover and cook over a low heat for 25 minutes or until the rice is tender and all the liquid is absorbed. Place a warm serving dish upside down over the casserole and invert the rice and chicken onto the serving dish.

BAGHDAD CHICKEN AND RICE

This Iraqi dish is basically a pie filled with chicken pilav. Prepare chicken, rice, and orange pilav as described in the recipe above plus 1 pound shortcrust pastry. Roll out the pastry and line a deep ovenproof pie dish with it, leaving enough pastry for the cover. Fill the dish with the rice and chicken and cover the top with pastry. Seal and pattern the edges and make two cuts in the center of the pie top. Bake in a preheated oven at 400° F for 30 minutes or until the pastry is nicely browned and cooked.

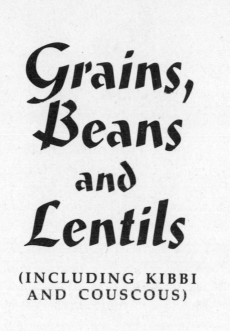

Grains, Beans and Lentils

(INCLUDING KIBBI
AND COUSCOUS)

Rice
Yellow Rice
Iraqi Steamed Rice
Lentil and Rice Pilav
Lentil, Rice, and Spinach
    Pilav
Rice with Fava Beans
Lentils and Noodles in Butter
Rice with Noodles
Rice, Noodles, and Lentils
    with Tomato Sauce
Burghul Wheat: Dry
    Roasted, Fried
Simple Burghul Pilav
Burghul Wheat and Eggplant
    Pilav
Burghul Wheat and Lamb
    Stew

Basic Kibbi
Raw Kibbi
Fried Kibbi
Stuffed Kibbi
Kibbi Baked on a Tray
Couscous
Couscous with Sweet
    Moroccan Sauce
Lentils and Spinach
Spiced Lamb and Chick-Pea
    Casserole
Arabian Apple Beanpot
Hot Lentil Pot
Lentils Baked with Noodles
Fresh Bean Casserole

The Arabic diet is a healthful one in which grains and beans play an important part. Wheat, rice, lentils, chick-peas, and other beans are basic elements of the cuisine. Apart from bread flour there are three other important wheat products. First, burghul (bulgur) or cracked wheat, a delicious grain used in the same way as rice and also one of the main ingredients of *kibbi*, the national dish of Syria and Lebanon. Second, couscous, the national dish of Morocco, Tunisia, and Algeria, and third, wheat-flour noodles which are usually served cooked with rice or lentils or both. Rice, cooked by a variety of methods, is served on its own or as a pilav in which it is cooked with a small or large and exotic selection of other ingredients. Beans, particularly lentils and chick-peas, are cooked with rice or wheat products or served on their own, cold or hot, with a dressing of olive oil and lemon juice. They are also puréed to make dips (see Mezze chapter) or added to casseroles of meat and/or vegetables.

This chapter is divided into four sections in which rice, burghul wheat (including *kibbi*), couscous, and beans are each discussed separately.

Rice (Roz)

Rice, along with bread, is part of the staple diet of the Arab world. It is served plain, boiled or steamed with salt and butter or oil, or as a pilav in which it is cooked together with a small or wide variety of other ingredients. Traditionally a pilav is served by inverting the cooking pot on a serving dish and leaving it to stand for a few moments. In this way the dish is layered in the order it was cooked—meat first, vegetables second, and rice third. Plain boiled rice may be colored yellow with turmeric or saffron and is often garnished with pine nuts or other nuts fried in oil or butter, or with a sauce. It is served at the table together with all the other dishes and is treated as another dish rather than as an accompaniment. Each country or even region has its own particular way of cooking rice, and each has its own merits, but they are all variations on a basic theme, so I have restricted the methods given here to two of the most popular and to a third, exclusive to Iraqi cooking, which I like particularly.

RICE

METHOD I

Serves 4

Popular in Lebanon, Syria, and Jordan. Quantities are given in volumes, since it is the volume of water relative to the volume of rice that is important, rather than weight.

1½ cups long-grain or Basmati rice
2 cups cold water
2 tablespoons butter or margarine or oil

1 teaspoon salt
2 tablespoons pine nuts or other nuts, chopped if large
2 tablespoons butter or oil

Put the rice in a colander and wash under running water until the water runs clear. Now leave the rice to drain completely. Bring the water, butter (or margarine or oil) and salt to the boil in a heavy pan. Stir in the rice and return to the boil. Reduce the heat, cover the pan with a tight-fitting lid, and simmer for 20 minutes. The rice should now be tender, the grains separate, and all the water absorbed. Leave the pan covered, remove it from the heat, and leave it to stand for 10 minutes. Just before the rice is finished, fry the nuts in the oil or butter until nicely browned. Transfer the rice to a serving bowl, pour the fried nuts and oil they were cooked in over the rice, and serve.

METHOD II

Serves 4

Popular in Egypt. Quantities as in Method I but use boiling, not cold water.

Put the rice in a colander and wash under running water until the water runs clear. Leave the rice to drain completely. Heat the butter (or margarine or oil) in a heavy pan, add the rice, and sauté, while stirring, for 2–3 minutes, covering all the grains with the fat. Remove the pan from the heat and pour in the boiling water. Add the salt, stir well, and return to the heat. Bring to the boil, reduce the heat, cover with a tight-fitting lid, and simmer for 20 minutes. Leave the pan covered, remove it from the heat, and leave to stand for 10 minutes. Just before the rice is finished, fry the nuts in the fat until they are nicely browned. Transfer the rice to a serving bowl, pour the fried nuts and oil they were cooked in over it, and serve.

YELLOW RICE

For yellow rice add ½ teaspoon of turmeric or powdered saffron to the pot at the start of the cooking time in Method I or fry with the rice in Method II (see preceding directions).

VARIATIONS ON METHOD I OR II
1. Toss into the cooked rice ¾ cup raisins, presoaked in hot water and drained, and garnish the cooked rice with fried onions as well as nuts.
2. Boil the rice in vegetable or meat stock instead of plain water.
3. For different-flavored rice try adding ½–1 teaspoon of one or more of the following spices to the pot at the start of the cooking time in Method I or fry with the rice in Method II: curry powder, cinnamon, cardamom.

IRAQI STEAMED RICE

Serves 4 or 5

This method of cooking rice is very similar to that used to make Iranian *chelo*, the aim being to form a thin golden crust of rice at the bottom of the pan. This is loosened off after cooking and used to garnish the steamed rice.

2 cups Basmati or long-grain rice	6 cups boiling water
6 tablespoons unsalted butter	1 tablespoon salt

Put the rice in a colander and wash under running water until the water runs clear. Leave the rice to drain completely. Heat one-third of the butter in a heavy pot, add the rice, and stir over high heat for 2–3 minutes. Pour in the boiling water, stir in the salt, return to the boil, and gently boil for 6–7 minutes. Drain the rice off and discard the cooking liquid. Put half of the remaining butter in the heavy pot and gently melt it. Add the drained rice and distribute it evenly in the pot. Melt the remaining butter and pour it over the rice. Cover the pot with a tight-fitting lid and cook over a medium heat for 5 minutes. Reduce the heat to very low and cook for a further 30 minutes. Tip out the rice, scrape the crust from the bottom of the pan, and garnish the rice with it. If your pan is likely to stick put the base in cold water for 5 minutes at the end of the cooking period, which helps to loosen the crust.

LENTIL AND RICE PILAV
(Mujaddarah)

Serves 6

This is a popular dish throughout the Middle East. It is cheap to make and provides a healthful combination of foodstuffs. It is usually served topped with yogurt and fried onions, although you may also serve it with a tomato sauce and fried onion topping. The proportions of rice to lentils used is very much up to personal taste. I have used equal amounts of each.

1 cup brown lentils, picked over for stones, cleaned, and soaked for at least 2 hours
3 medium onions, 1 finely diced and 2 finely sliced
½ cup olive or other vegetable oil

1 cup long-grain rice
salt and black pepper
2 cloves garlic
½ teaspoon allspice
1 cup plain yogurt

Drain the lentils, put them in a pot with 2½ cups fresh water, cover, and gently boil for 20 minutes. Fry the diced onion golden brown in one-quarter of the oil. Stir the onion into the lentils, then add the rice, salt, and pepper. Stir well, bring to the boil, reduce the heat to a simmer, cover the pot, and cook for 20 minutes or until the rice and lentils are tender and all the water is absorbed. Check the pot toward the end of the cooking period to see that there is enough water to keep the contents moist. Add a little water if needed. Fry the sliced onions and garlic in the remaining oil until dark brown in color. Stir in the allspice. Put the rice and lentils in a mound on a serving dish. Make a depression in the top of the mound and pour in the yogurt. Sprinkle the fried onions and garlic over the top and serve hot or cold as a main meal or side dish.

LENTIL, RICE, AND SPINACH PILAV

Serves 6

Ingredients as for lentil and rice pilav above, plus:

1 *pound fresh spinach, washed and*   3 *tablespoons melted butter* or *olive oil*
chopped, or 8 ounces frozen spinach,
defrosted and drained

Follow the instructions for preparing lentil and rice pilav and while the rice and lentils are cooking sauté the spinach in the butter or oil until it is wilted. Gently stir the spinach into the cooked rice and lentils and proceed as directed in the above recipe.

RICE WITH FAVA (BROAD) BEANS
(Roz ou Ful)
EGYPT

Serves 4

2 *tablespoons olive oil* or *other oil*   8 *ounces fresh fava (broad) beans,*
2 *cloves garlic, put through a garlic*   *shelled (if young and tender keep the*
  press   *pods and chop them into thirds), or*
1 *medium onion, sliced*   *use frozen or canned beans*
½ *teaspoon allspice*   1½ *cups boiling water*
½ *teaspoon ground coriander*   1 *cup long-grain rice, washed and*
                                   drained
                                salt and black pepper

Heat the oil in a heavy pot and lightly brown the garlic and onion in it. Stir in the spices and beans (and chopped pods if used) and pour in the boiling water. Simmer for 15 minutes or until the beans are tender. Add the rice, bring to the boil, reduce the heat, season to taste with salt and pepper, cover, and simmer for 20 minutes or until the rice is cooked and the water absorbed. Invert the pot over a serving dish. Remove the pot, leaving a mound of rice topped with beans.

PASTA DISHES

Pasta, perhaps brought back from Italy many centuries ago, is used in Arabic cooking normally in conjunction with rice or lentils or both. Like the Chinese, some Arabs eat noodles on New Year's Eve when the long noodles become symbols of hoped-for longevity.

LENTILS AND NOODLES IN BUTTER
SYRIA

Serves 4 as main course, 6 as side dish

Serve as a side dish to main meals or as a simple main dish.

1 cup brown lentils	*2 medium onions, finely diced*
salt and black pepper	*½ teaspoon ground coriander*
1 cup thin noodles	*¼–½ teaspoon cayenne pepper*
½ cup butter, melted	*1 teaspoon dried basil*

Wash and drain the lentils and put them in a heavy pot. Cover with water, add salt to taste, and bring to the boil. Reduce the heat, cover, and simmer for 1 hour or until the lentils are just tender. Drain and set aside. Meanwhile put the noodles in a large pan of salted boiling water and cook, stirring, until just tender. Drain and reserve. In a large heavy frying pan melt half the butter and fry the onions until softened and lightly browned. Stir in the spices and basil and cook a further 2 minutes. Mix in the cooked lentils and noodles, season to taste with salt and pepper, and heat through. Pour the remaining hot melted butter over the food and serve.

RICE WITH NOODLES
(Roz bel Shaghia)
EGYPT

Serves 4

Serves as a side dish to a main meal.

4 tablespoons sesame seed oil
1 medium onion, finely diced
1 clove garlic, put through a garlic press
½ teaspoon turmeric
1½ cups long-grain rice

½ cup thin noodles broken into pieces
4 tablespoons raisins, plumped up in hot water and drained (optional)
2 cups boiling water
salt and black pepper

Heat the oil in a large heavy frying pan and sauté the onion and garlic until just softened. Stir in the turmeric and then the rice and noodles. Stir and gently cook until the rice and pasta are coated in oil and lightly browned. Add the raisins if used, pour in the boiling water, and season with salt and pepper. Reduce the heat to very low and simmer until the rice is tender and all the liquid absorbed. If the pot contents dry out during cooking, add a little more water.

RICE, NOODLES, AND LENTILS WITH TOMATO SAUCE
(Koushari)
EGYPT

Serves 4

This Egyptian recipe makes a substantial meal. Serve with a fresh crisp green salad and a bowl of plain yogurt.

Follow the rice with noodles recipe above but use 1 cup rice and 1 cup noodles. At the end of the cooking time fold into the rice and noodles 1 cup cooked, drained brown lentils. Transfer to a serving dish and serve topped with the following tomato sauce.

1 medium onion, finely diced
2 cloves garlic, put through a garlic press

2 tablespoons sesame seed oil
3 tablespoons tomato purée
salt and black pepper to taste

Sauté the onion and garlic in the oil until softened and lightly browned. Stir in the tomato purée, 1¼ cups water, and seasoning. Mix well, bring to the boil, reduce the heat, and simmer for a few minutes. Remove from the heat and use.

BURGHUL WHEAT

Burghul, also called bulgur, bulgar, or cracked wheat, is prepared by parboiling whole-wheat grains in a minimum amount of water. The wheat is then spread out in the sun, dried, and finally cracked between stone rollers. Burghul is the second most common product of Middle Eastern wheat crops, flour being the first. It has an enjoyable, distinctive taste and lends itself to many ways of cooking. Probably the best-known burghul dishes are tabbouleh (see page 30) and *kibbi*, the national dish of Syria and Lebanon described later in this chapter.

Burghul is cooked by steaming or boiling after first dry roasting or frying it in oil. It is used in the same way as rice, as an accompaniment to other dishes or in the preparation of pilav. It can be crushed to varying degrees of fineness and is sold in various grades. The finest-ground is used to make *kibbi*, the medium for tabbouleh and ordinary cooking, and the coarse for making pilavs or for addition to casseroles and stews.

For additional information on burghul, see page xxv.

BURGHUL
DRY ROASTING METHOD

Serves 6

1 pound burghul wheat	*salt*
water or stock	

Measure the volume of the burghul in cups and then pour it into a dry, heavy saucepan over a medium heat and cook (this is called dry roasting) while stirring for 2–3 minutes. Remove from the heat and pour in twice the volume of water or stock as burghul. Add salt to taste. Return to the boil, reduce the heat to a very low simmer, cover, and cook gently for 20–25 minutes or until all the liquid is absorbed and the wheat is tender.

FRYING METHOD

Serves 6

½ cup butter	*water or stock*
1 medium onion, finely chopped	*salt and black pepper*
1 pound burghul wheat	

Melt the butter in a heavy pan and sauté the onion until well softened. Measure the burghul by volume and then stir it into the pan. Cook and stir for 2–3 minutes and pour in twice the volume of water or stock. Add salt and pepper to taste, bring to the boil, reduce the heat to very low, simmer, and cook gently for 20–25 minutes or until all the liquid is absorbed and the wheat is tender.

Serving Serve the burghul topped with 4 tablespoons pine nuts lightly fried in a little butter, and a bowl of plain yogurt for spooning over to taste.

SIMPLE BURGHUL PILAV

Follow the frying method above but fry 4 tablespoons pine nuts or blanched almonds with the onions. Combine ½ cup of raisins, previously plumped up in hot water, with the burghul before adding it to the pot. Follow the recipe as directed.

BURGHUL WHEAT AND EGGPLANT PILAV
SYRIA AND LEBANON

Serves 6

Ingredients as for preparing burghul wheat by frying method (see above) plus:

2 medium eggplants, cubed	*4 tablespoons butter*
salt	*3 tablespoons chopped parsley*

Salt the eggplants and set them aside in a colander for 30 minutes. Meanwhile prepare the burghul by the frying method. Rinse the eggplants in cold water and pat dry on absorbent paper. Cook them in the butter, turning, until they are tender, and then stir in the parsley. Fold this mixture into the burghul and serve. For a variation, fold grated cheese into the burghul wheat at the same time as the eggplant mixture.

BURGHUL WHEAT AND LAMB STEW
SYRIA AND LEBANON

Serves 4

Serve with plain yogurt and salad.

2 medium onions, finely chopped	½ teaspoon ground cinnamon
1 cup butter	½ teaspoon allspice
1 pound lean stewing lamb, cubed	½ teaspoon cumin
½ cup chick-peas, soaked overnight and drained	salt and black pepper
2 tablespoons tomato purée	1 cup burghul wheat

Fry the onion in half the butter until lightly browned. Add the meat and fry, stirring, until it is well browned all over. Stir in the chick-peas, tomato purée, spices, and seasoning to taste, cover with water, and bring to the boil. Reduce the heat, cover, and simmer for 1 hour or until the meat is not quite tender. Keep the meat covered in water during cooking. Melt the remaining butter over medium heat in another pan and stir the burghul wheat in it until each grain is coated. Pour in the contents of the pan containing the meat. Cover and cook, with occasional stirring, over a low heat for 15–20 minutes or until the burghul is tender.

KIBBI
SYRIA AND LEBANON

The basic ingredients of *kibbi* are fine burghul wheat and finely ground lean lamb. They are pounded together to form a paste which is then formed into various shapes, stuffed with a meat and nut mixture, and eaten raw, deep fried, or layered in trays and baked. The best meat to use is leg of lamb, trimmed of all fat before double grinding. The traditional preparation of basic *kibbi* requires long work with the *madaqua* (pestle) and *jorn* (mortar), but nowadays an electric blender or a food processor makes the work much easier. The recipes given are for the basic *kibbi* and meat stuffing. Instructions are then given on how to put them together to make *kibbi nayye*, fried *kibbi*, *kibbi* balls, and baked *kibbi*.

For cooked *kibbi* dishes, the basic *kibbi* and the basic stuffing could be prepared as much as a day ahead and combined as instructed only when needed. *Kibbi* that is to be served raw, however, should always be made just before serving.

BASIC KIBBI

¾ cup fine burghul wheat
iced water
2 medium onions, grated or finely chopped
1 teaspoon salt

½ teaspoon cinnamon
½ teaspoon allspice
¼ teaspoon black pepper
12 ounces lamb, finely ground

Cover the burghul wheat in iced water and leave it to soak for 10 minutes. Drain and press the burghul between the palms of your hands to remove as much excess water as possible. Put the onions, salt, and spices in a blender or food processor with a little iced water and blend to a thick paste. Combine this with the meat and in small amounts put the mixture through the blender or processor again. Now add this paste to the burghul and again put this new mixture through the blender or processor to form a smooth paste. Alternatively, for the traditional method, follow the same procedure as above but using a pestle and mortar. The *kibbi* paste is now ready for use in the following recipes.

BASIC KIBBI STUFFING

4 tablespoons pine nuts or chopped walnuts
2 tablespoons butter
1 medium onion, finely diced

8 ounces lamb, ground
¼ teaspoon cinnamon
¼ teaspoon allspice
salt and black pepper

Fry the nuts in the butter until lightly browned. Add the onions and cook until softened. Stir in the meat, spices, and seasoning and fry, stirring and pressing (to keep the meat from forming into lumps), until the meat is browned. The stuffing is now ready for use. See recipes below.

RAW KIBBI
(Kibbi Nayye)

Serves 4

basic kibbi *(see above)*
3 tablespoons olive oil
1 bunch scallions, chopped
sprigs of fresh mint

lemon wedges
1 head crisp Romaine lettuce, leaves
  separated
pita bread

Form the *kibbi* into a mound on a large plate. Dip your fingers in iced water and make a well in the center of the mound. Make shallow channels like spokes in a wheel from the center well to the circumference. Drizzle olive oil in the well and the channels. Garnish with scallions, mint, and lemon wedges, and serve with lettuce leaves and pita bread, pieces of which are used to scoop up the *kibbi*.

FRIED KIBBI

Serves 4

basic kibbi *(see above)*
oil for frying

Dip your hands in iced water and form the *kibbi* into patties or hamburger shapes. Fry on both sides in shallow oil until browned and cooked right through.

STUFFED KIBBI
(Kibbeyet)

Serves 6 to 8

Serve this hot or cold as part of a mezze or with salad, bread, and yogurt as a main meal.

basic kibbi *(see above)*
basic kibbi *stuffing (see above)*
½ cup butter, melted

Preheat the oven to 350° F. Pinch off a lump of *kibbi* the size of a small egg and roll it between your palms into an oval shape about 4 inches long. Dip your index finger into iced water and make a hollow in the oval cake by slowly pushing and pulling your finger down one end while holding the wall together with the palm of your other hand. Seal any cracks with a wet finger. Fill the hollow with stuffing and seal over the end with a wet hand. Grease a baking tray with half the butter and place the stuffed *kibbi* side by side on the tray. Brush them with the remaining melted butter and bake in the preheated oven for 20–25 minutes or until they are golden brown. Alternatively the stuffed *kibbi* can be deep fried in hot oil until golden brown.

KIBBI BAKED ON A TRAY
(Kibbi bil Sanieh)

Serves 6 to 8

Serve hot or cold with salads, yogurt, and bread.

basic kibbi *(see above)*
basic kibbi *stuffing (see above)*
4 tablespoons butter, melted

Preheat the oven to 375° F. Brush a shallow baking dish or tray with half the butter and spread half the basic *kibbi* on the bottom. Spread all the stuffing on this and finish off with a topping of the remaining *kibbi*. Brush with the remaining butter. Cut a diamond pattern into the top of the *kibbi*, using diagonal knife strokes, and then bake in the preheated oven for 40–45 minutes or until it is nicely browned and crisp.

COUSCOUS
NORTH AFRICA

Couscous is the name of a product made from fine semolina (which itself is made from wheat grain) and it is also the name of the dish which includes couscous as the main ingredient. Couscous is the national dish of North Africa, but it is also popular in Egypt, where it is more often served with a sweet sauce and eaten as a dessert than as a main dish. The famous North African dish consists of a steaming mound of couscous with chunks of lamb and vegetables on top and a rich sauce poured over.

Couscous grain can now be bought in packets from Greek or other foreign produce stores. It is satisfactory and easy to use, but for those of you who have the time and patience I have given, below, instructions on how to make your own couscous. *Harissa* (see page xxvi), a hot pepper sauce, is traditionally used with couscous. It is either cooked with the meat and vegetable stew or served as a side dish to be added to taste by each individual.

The basic steps in the preparation of couscous are as follows:

1. Make or buy couscous.
2. Make or buy *harissa*.
3. Prepare the meat and vegetable sauce.
4. Steam the couscous over the sauce until it is cooked. (Couscous is never cooked in the sauce.) There is a special pot for this called a couscousier, designed to cook the stew and steam the couscous at the same time. It is basically a saucepan with a snug-fitting colander on top—an arrangement that is fine as a substitute for the real thing.
5. Finally the couscous grains are piled on a large serving dish, the meat and vegetables lifted out of the pan and arranged over the grains. Some of the cooking broth or sauce is poured over the top and the remainder is served in a side bowl.
6. Sometimes the finished couscous is topped with a sweet sauce which contrasts well with the spicy meat broth. The recipe given later for sweet Moroccan sauce can be used for this purpose.

TO MAKE COUSCOUS GRAINS

This recipe makes enough couscous for 12 servings and any unused can be stored in a dry container. Initially, however, couscous is easier to make in small quantities, so for the first time you try it, halve the quantities given.

1½ pounds fine semolina *1 cup plain flour*
1 teaspoon salt *up to 1 cup cold water*

Place the semolina in a large bowl and form a well in the center. Combine the salt and the flour. Put about 2 tablespoons of water in the well and gently push in semolina from the sides. Now with a circular motion use the palm of your hand to evenly spread the moistened semolina. Sprinkle over this one-third to half of the flour-salt mixture and gently mix it in with the same hand motion. As you start to coat the semolina grains with the flour-salt mixture, small grains of couscous will form. Sprinkle in a little more water and flour-salt mixture and continue the process. Now turn the contents of the bowl into a large, medium- or coarse-meshed sieve and sift out the couscous grains. The finer material will go through and you can pick out any large lumps of conglomerate material, leaving only the couscous grains. Return the lumpy bits to the bowl, breaking up any large lumps, and repeat the original process until all the semolina is used up. Steam the prepared couscous grains in a colander or couscousier over boiling water for 10 minutes, then spread them out on a dry cloth, gently break up any lumps that have formed, and leave the couscous to dry out in a warm airy place. Finally store the couscous in a dry container.

TO MAKE COUSCOUS

Serves 6

This is a recipe that you may add to or change to include any suitable vegetables, meat, or poultry that you have available. The thing to remember is to bear in mind the relative cooking times of each ingredient and to add them at the appropriate time.

1 pound lamb, cut into 1½-inch cubes
2 medium onions, chopped
4 tablespoons butter or olive oil
½ teaspoon saffron or turmeric
1 teaspoon ground ginger
1½ teaspoons freshly ground black pepper
salt to taste
2 tablespoons chopped fresh parsley and/or coriander leaves
water or stock
1 cup chick-peas, soaked overnight, drained (or use canned cooked chick-peas)

4 medium carrots, thinly sliced lengthwise
4 small turnips, peeled and quartered
4 small zucchini, chopped into quarters
1 pound couscous
4 tablespoons pine nuts or almonds or chopped walnuts
1 tablespoon butter or oil
¾ cup raisins, soaked in hot water, drained
harissa sauce (see page xxvi)

Put the lamb, onions, butter or oil, spices, and 2 teaspoons of salt and the herbs in the bottom of the couscousier or heavy pan (on which a colander can fit snugly) and gently cook, while stirring, for 10 minutes. Add enough water or stock to cover the meat and add the drained chick-peas (leave this for later if using canned chick-peas). Bring to the boil, reduce the heat, cover the pan, and simmer for 1 hour. Adjust the seasoning for taste, and add the carrots and turnips. Continue cooking for 20 minutes and then add the zucchini, and canned chick-peas if used. The stew is ready when both the meat and vegetables are tender (another 10–13 minutes). Meanwhile the couscous is prepared. Place the couscous in a large bowl and gently stir in 2 cups cold water. Immediately drain it away and allow the wet grains to stand for 10–15 minutes. As they well up rake them with your fingers to break up any lumps that form. Turn the grains into a colander or the top of the couscousier and place them over the cooking stew for 30 minutes before serving. If steam escapes from between the pan and steamer seal it with cheesecloth or foil. Near the end of the cooking period lightly brown the nuts in the tablespoon of butter or oil, then stir in the raisins and heat through. Finally if you want the stew to be very hot, stir in *harissa* to taste toward the end of the cooking period. If not, cook the *harissa* with 2–3 tablespoons of olive oil over a low heat for 5 minutes, and serve it as a side dish.

To serve the couscous pile the couscous grains from the steamer onto a large plate. Remove the meat and vegetables from the sauce with a slotted spoon and decorate the couscous with them. Pour half the cooking broth over the couscous and garnish with the fried nuts and raisins. Serve with a bowl of the remaining broth and a bowl of *harissa* sauce as side dishes.

Finally, for the coup de grace, you can, if you wish, pour sweet Moroccan sauce over the couscous. See recipe below.

VARIATIONS: Substitute beef or pieces of chicken for the lamb or use a combination of meat and poultry.

Fish can also be used. Use filleted fish and reduce the cooking time by half.

COUSCOUS WITH
SWEET MOROCCAN SAUCE

Serves 4

This dish is delicious on its own or just the sauce can be used in conjunction with the couscous recipe given below.

½ cup butter	½ teaspoon freshly ground black pepper
2 medium onions, diced	salt to taste
1 tablespoon cinnamon	⅔ cup sugar
½ teaspoon saffron or turmeric	1½ cups raisins, soaked in hot water
1 teaspoon ground ginger	and drained
4 tablespoons pine nuts or almonds	1 pound couscous

Melt the butter in a heavy pan and sauté the onion until it is just softened. Stir in the spices, nuts, and seasoning, and cook, stirring, for 2–3 minutes. Add 1½ cups water, sugar, and raisins and bring to the boil. Reduce the heat, cover, and simmer for 25–30 minutes. The sauce should be quite thick; if not, remove the cover and reduce the liquid over a moderate heat. Meanwhile prepare the couscous. Place the couscous in a large bowl and gently stir in 2 cups cold water. Immediately drain it away and allow the wet grains to stand for 10–15 minutes. As they swell up, rake them with your fingers to break up any lumps that form. Steam the couscous over boiling water for 30 minutes, or until tender. Pile the cooked grains on a serving dish, make a hollow in the top, fill with the sauce, and serve.

BEANS AND LENTILS

Apart from those given here, there are recipes throughout the book containing beans and lentils as ingredients, particularly in the chapters on mezze, and on meat and poultry dishes, and the preceding recipes of this chapter.

LENTILS AND SPINACH
(Adas be Sabanigh)
FERTILE CRESCENT

Serves 4

1 cup lentils, soaked and drained
1 pound spinach, washed and chopped or 8 ounces frozen spinach, defrosted, drained, and chopped
1 medium onion, finely chopped
2 cloves garlic, put through a garlic press

4 tablespoons butter
½ teaspoon ground cumin
½ teaspoon ground coriander
salt and black pepper
juice of 1 lemon
2 hard-boiled eggs, sliced

Cover the lentils with water and cook until tender. Cook the spinach until tender in a little water. Drain the lentils and spinach and combine together. Fry the onion and garlic golden brown in the butter in a large frying pan and stir in the cumin, coriander, salt, and pepper. Fry a further 2 minutes and then stir in the lentil and spinach mixture. Add the lemon juice and heat through, while stirring. Adjust the seasoning and serve garnished with slices of hard-boiled eggs. This dish is also good cold.

SPICED LAMB AND CHICK-PEA CASSEROLE
MOROCCO

Serves 4

This recipe uses a rich combination of spices and is complemented by the addition of strands of beaten egg made tart with fresh lemon juice. Serve with pita bread and a bowl of plain yogurt for spooning to taste.

2 tablespoons olive oil	1 teaspoon ground cinnamon
8 ounces lamb, cubed	½ teaspoon turmeric
2 medium onions, diced	¾ cup chick-peas, soaked overnight,
1 pound ripe tomatoes, peeled and chopped or 8 ounces canned tomatoes, chopped	drained
	¾ cup lentils, washed and drained
	salt and black pepper to taste
1 tablespoon chopped parsley	juice of 1 lemon
½ teaspoon ground coriander	2 eggs, beaten
1 teaspoon ground ginger	

Heat the oil in a heavy saucepan and brown the lamb on all sides. Add the onion and lightly sauté. Add the tomatoes, parsley, coriander, ginger, cinnamon, and turmeric, stir well and cook for 1–2 minutes. Stir in the chick-peas, add 4 cups water, lentils, salt, and pepper, and bring to the boil. Cover, reduce the heat, and simmer for 1 hour or until all the ingredients are tender. Stir the lemon juice into the beaten egg and gently beat the mixture into the stew with a fork to form strands of egg. Remove the pan from the heat and serve.

ARABIAN APPLE BEANPOT

Serves 6

This recipe is from *Middle Eastern Vegetarian Cookery*. With such an appropriate name, I couldn't leave it out of this book. Serve with a bowl of yogurt, chopped apricots, and boiled rice.

1 pound dried fava or butter beans, or other beans, soaked overnight and drained

2 tablespoons vegetable oil or butter

2 medium onions, sliced

2 medium cooking apples, cored and sliced

½ teaspoon turmeric

½ teaspoon ground allspice

½ teaspoon ground cinnamon

salt and black pepper

Put the beans and 5 cups water in a heavy saucepan and bring to the boil. Cover, reduce the heat, and simmer until the beans are tender— about 1½ hours. Heat the oil or butter in a large, heavy frying pan and sauté the onions until golden. Add the apple, turmeric, allspice, and cinnamon, and cook, stirring, until the apple is softened. Drain the beans and reserve the cooking liquid. Add the beans to the frying pan with just enough cooking liquid to wet the contents of the pan. Season to taste with salt and pepper and simmer for 1–2 minutes.

HOT LENTIL POT
ALGERIA

Serves 4 to 6

This is a colorful hotchpotch of browns, reds, and greens spiked with cayenne pepper. Add more or less cayenne than suggested in the recipe to suit your taste.

1 pound brown lentils, soaked 2–3 hours, drained

2 cloves garlic, put through a garlic press

2 medium onions, chopped

4 tablespoons butter

1 pound ripe tomatoes, peeled and chopped or 8 ounces canned tomatoes, chopped

2 medium green peppers, seeded, deribbed, and chopped

1 teaspoon paprika

½–1 teaspoon cayenne

salt and black pepper to taste

3 tablespoons chopped parsley and/or chopped mint

Cover the lentils in a minimum of water and cook uncovered until just tender. Add water as needed but aim to end the cooking period with the lentils just moist. Brown the garlic and onions in the butter in a heavy pot. Add the tomatoes, green pepper, paprika, and cayenne and cook for another 2–3 minutes while stirring. Pour in the lentils, season to taste with salt and pepper, cover, and simmer for 10 minutes. Remove from the heat and stir in the herbs.

LENTILS BAKED WITH NOODLES
(Rishta)
FERTILE CRESCENT

Serves 6

4 tablespoons butter	8 ounces noodles, cooked and drained
hot lentil pot (preceding recipe)	1 cup grated cheese

Preheat the oven to 375° F. Butter a baking dish and layer the noodles and hot lentil pot mixture, ending up with a layer of lentil pot. Sprinkle grated cheese over the top and bake for 30 minutes or until the cheese is nicely browned.

FRESH BEAN CASSEROLE
(Tajine Ful)
NORTH AFRICA

Serves 4

This North African dish can be used with any freshly shelled beans, peas, or green beans. It follows the normal practice of Moroccan cooking of directly boiling the meat without prefrying.

1½ pounds lamb, cubed	½ teaspoon ground ginger
2 cloves garlic, put through a garlic press	½ teaspoon turmeric
2 medium onions, chopped	salt and black pepper
4 tablespoons olive oil	1 pound shelled beans, peas, or green beans, topped and tailed
1 teaspoon coriander seeds, crushed	

Put the cubed lamb in a bowl, mix in the garlic and onions, cover the bowl, and set aside for 20 minutes. Heat the oil gently in a heavy pan and stir in the coriander, ginger, and turmeric. Mix well and pour in a little water. Bring to the boil and stir in the lamb, onion, and garlic mixture. Cover with water, season to taste with salt and pepper, bring to the boil, reduce the heat, cover, and simmer for 1 hour or until the lamb is tender. Meanwhile cook the beans in a little water until just tender but still firm. Drain and toward the end of the cooking period of the lamb stir in the beans. Adjust the seasoning. Serve when the meat is tender.

Stuffed Vegetables

(MISHSHI)

Fillings and Sauces for
   Stuffing Vegetables
Stuffed Eggplants
Stuffed Zucchini
Stuffed Red or Green Peppers
Stuffed Squash
Stuffed Tomatoes

Stuffed Onions
Stuffed Potatoes
Stuffed Artichokes
Stuffed Apples
Stuffed Fennel
Stuffed Vine Leaves,
   Cabbage, and Swiss Chard

S tuffed vegetables, called *mishshi* or dolmas, are an intrinsic part of
Arabic cuisine, and nearly every vegetable available to the Middle
Eastern cook has been adapted to this way of cooking. There are a host
of fillings and as many ways of stuffing and cooking the vegetables. To
simplify matters I have decided to give recipes for five different fillings,
two with meat and three without, plus a description of how to prepare
and cook a variety of vegetables suitable for stuffing. Finally there are
recipes for tomato sauce and yogurt sauce which may be substituted for
water as the cooking medium and for a *mishshi* garnish. Thus you can
select a filling, a vegetable, and a sauce in whichever combination appeals
to you and make your own *mishshi*. Zucchini, eggplant, green or red
peppers, and vine or cabbage leaves are the most common vegetables
used for stuffing. Most *mishshi* can be served hot, warm, or cold. If you
plan to serve them warm or cold use olive oil for any frying that is
required, since this is the most digestible oil eaten cold. Serve with rice,
salad, and pickles.

FILLINGS FOR STUFFING
VEGETABLES

The amounts given provide enough filling for preparing stuffed vegetables for 4 to 6 people. These fillings can be prepared 3–4 hours before
they are to be used.

MEAT FILLING

2 tablespoons olive oil or *melted butter*

2 *medium onions, finely diced*

2 *cloves garlic, put through a garlic press*

1 *pound lamb, or* beef *or cooked chicken, ground*

4 *tablespoons pine nuts or* whole *blanched almonds or chopped walnuts*

½ *teaspoon allspice*

1 *teaspoon cinnamon*

2 *tablespoons freshly chopped parsley or mint or* coriander

salt and black pepper to taste

Heat the oil or melted butter in a heavy frying pan and add the onions and garlic. Fry until golden, while stirring, and then add the meat. Fry and stir, making sure no lumps form, until the meat is browned. Add the remaining ingredients, mix well, and cook over a low heat for a further 5 minutes. Cool and the filling is ready.

MEAT AND RICE FILLING

12 *ounces lamb or* beef *or cooked chicken, ground*

½ *cup long-grain rice, washed*

½ *teaspoon turmeric*

¼ *teaspoon nutmeg*

½ *teaspoon allspice*

1 *tablespoon melted butter*

1 *tablespoon tomato purée*

salt and black pepper to taste

Combine all ingredients and mix well together. The rice is left uncooked because the meat shrinks during cooking, leaving space for the rice to expand.

RICE FILLING

In these recipes cooked rice has been used, but if the vegetables you are stuffing have a long cooking time use uncooked rice and reduce the amount used to half that of the cooked rice, and pack the vegetables less tightly.

2 medium onions, finely diced
2 tablespoons olive oil
5 cups cooked long-grain rice
2 medium tomatoes, peeled and chopped
2 tablespoons freshly chopped parsley or
    mint or coriander

½ teaspoon allspice
½ teaspoon cinnamon
salt and black pepper to taste
4 tablespoons raisins, presoaked and
    drained (optional)

Lightly fry the onions in the oil, then combine it with all the other ingredients and mix well.

VARIATIONS: Replace half the rice in the above recipe with 3 cups cooked and drained chick-peas.

Substitute the tomatoes in the recipe for rice filling (above) with about 1 cup nuts, e.g. pine nuts, blanched almonds, chopped walnuts, pistachios.

RICE AND DRIED FRUIT FILLING

Any combination of dried fruits may be used in this recipe.

1 medium onion, diced
2 tablespoons olive oil
5 cups cooked long-grain rice
¾ cup raisins, presoaked and drained
½ cup dried fruits, presoaked, drained,
    and chopped

juice of 1 lemon
1 tablespoon freshly chopped mint or 1
    teaspoon dried mint
½ teaspoon cinnamon
½ teaspoon allspice
salt and black pepper to taste

Lightly fry the onion in the oil, then combine it with all the other ingredients and mix well.

TOMATO FILLING

This is the filling used for the famous stuffed eggplant dish *imam bayldi*.

2 cloves garlic, put through a garlic
    press
2 medium onions, diced
2 tablespoons olive oil
4 medium tomatoes, peeled and chopped

1 teaspoon sugar
½ teaspoon dried oregano
juice of 1 lemon
2 tablespoons chopped parsley
salt and black pepper to taste

Lightly fry the garlic and onion in the oil. Transfer them to a bowl and add the remaining ingredients. Mix well.

TOMATO SAUCE

Makes 2½ cups

2 tablespoons olive oil or *melted butter*
2 medium onions, *finely chopped*
4 cloves garlic, *put through a garlic press*
1 cup chopped fresh or *canned tomatoes*

4 tablespoons tomato purée
1 teaspoon crushed oregano
½ teaspoon cinnamon
salt and black pepper to taste

Heat the oil or butter in a heavy frying pan and sauté the onions, and garlic until softened. Add the remaining ingredients and 1 cup water, mix well, bring to the boil, and gently simmer for 5 minutes.

QUICK TOMATO SAUCE

Makes 1½ cups

2 tablespoons tomato purée
juice of 1 lemon
salt and black pepper to taste

Combine all the ingredients with 1¼ cups water in a pan and bring to the boil. Remove from the heat and it's ready to use.

STABILIZED YOGURT SAUCE

Makes 2 cups

Cows'-milk yogurt curdles if it is cooked for any length of time or if it is boiled. Thus, unless it is going to be added to a dish just before it is to be served, it must be stabilized for use as a cooking sauce. This is not the case with goats'-milk yogurt, which curdles much less readily, particularly if salted.

 2 cups plain yogurt
 1 egg white
 ½ teaspoon salt

Put the yogurt into a small heavy pan, beat the egg white until it is just frothy, and stir it over a low heat into the yogurt along with the salt. Continue stirring, always in the same direction, until the mixture just boils. Reduce the heat to very low and leave it to simmer uncovered for 5 minutes or until it has become thick. The yogurt may now be cooked without curdling.

GARNISH FOR STUFFED VEGETABLES

½ teaspoon salt
2 cloves garlic, put through a garlic press

1 teaspoon dried crushed mint
juice of 1 lemon

In a pestle and mortar crush together the salt, garlic, and mint. Stir in the lemon juice and sprinkle the mixture over hot stuffed vegetables before serving.

VARIATION: If there is no time to make the above garnish just sprinkle the cooked dish of stuffed vegetables with fresh lemon juice and/or chopped fresh herbs or crushed dried herbs.

PREPARING AND COOKING STUFFED VEGETABLES

STUFFED EGGPLANTS

Serves 4

4 medium eggplants, stalks left on
salt
2 tablespoons olive oil or melted butter

selected filling (see preceding recipes)
water or tomato sauce or yogurt sauce
  (see recipes)

Wash the eggplants complete with stalks and make a deep slit from one end to the other without actually breaking open the end. Press open the slit and sprinkle liberally with salt. Set the eggplants aside for 30 minutes, then rinse them out and pat them dry on paper towels. Preheat the oven to 350° F. Heat the oil or butter in a heavy frying pan and fry the eggplants all over until they have softened but have not lost their shape. Grease a casserole dish and put the eggplants into it, open side up. Pack them with the selected filling and pour into the dish enough water or sauce to come halfway up the sides of the eggplants. Bake for 35–40 minutes or until the eggplants are soft.

STUFFED ZUCCHINI

Serves 4

2 pounds medium-size zucchini,
  washed
salt

selected filling (see preceding recipes)
2 cups water or tomato sauce or yogurt
  sauce (see recipes)

Cut the stem ends off the zucchini and carefully hollow out the center of each with an apple corer, leaving a ⅛–¼-inch shell all around.

Soak the hollowed zucchini in salted water for 10 minutes, then drain. Stuff them with the filling and then arrange them in a heavy casserole. Add the water or selected sauce and bring the pot to the boil. Cover, reduce the heat, and simmer for 30 minutes or until the zucchini are tender.

STUFFED RED OR GREEN PEPPERS

Serves 4

4 medium peppers, red or green
2 tablespoons olive oil
selected filling (see preceding recipes)

2 cups water or tomato sauce (see recipe)

Cut the tops off the peppers, and remove the seeds and the pith. Heat the oil in a heavy frying pan and lightly sauté the peppers all over until they are softened but still retain their shape. Preheat the oven to 350° F. Stuff the peppers with the selected filling and pack them into a casserole dish. Put the tops back on the peppers and pour into the dish the water or tomato sauce. Bake in the preheated oven for 30 minutes or until the peppers and filling are tender.

STUFFED SQUASH

Serves 4 to 6

Acorn, butternut, or Hubbard squash may be used.

1 large squash (1–1½ pounds), cut lengthwise in 2 and then crosswise in 2, seeds scraped out
salt
butter

selected filling (see preceding recipes)
2 cups water or tomato or yogurt sauce (see recipes)
juice of 1 lemon (optional)

Put the squash pieces or boats into a large pan of salted boiling water and cook until the pulp is just softened. Drain them and scoop out enough pulp to leave a thick shell. Preheat the oven to 350° F. Put the squash into a buttered baking dish and stuff with the selected filling. Pour the water (if water is used add the juice of 1 lemon as well) or sauce into the baking dish and bake in the preheated oven for 45 minutes or until the squash and filling are tender.

STUFFED TOMATOES

Serves 4

8 medium tomatoes
salt and black pepper to taste

selected filling (see preceding recipes)
2 tablespoons olive oil

Cut ¼–½-inch tops off the tomatoes and reserve them. Carefully scoop out the tomato pulp, leaving a ½-inch shell. Sprinkle the inside with salt and pepper and set aside. Chop the pulp and add to the filling. Stuff the tomatoes with the selected filling and brush them all over with olive oil. Put them in a shallow baking dish and replace the tops. Bake in a preheated oven at 350° F for 20 minutes.

STUFFED ONIONS

Serves 4

4 large onions, peeled
selected filling, (see preceding recipes)
juice of 1 lemon

Cook the onions in a small amount of water over low heat for 20 minutes. Drain and reserve the liquid. Cut a slice off the stem end of each onion and scoop out the centers, leaving a moderately thick wall. Stuff the onions with the selected filling. Set aside. Chop up the centers and place them in a baking dish along with the reserved liquid and the juice of 1 lemon. Pack the stuffed onions into the dish, cover, and bake in a preheated oven at 350° F for 1 hour or simmer, covered, over low heat on top of the stove for the same time.

STUFFED POTATOES

Serves 4

8 medium potatoes, peeled   *2 large tomatoes, sliced*
selected filling (see preceding recipes)   *water or tomato sauce*

Working from an end, hollow out each potato with a sharp knife or spoon or apple corer, leaving a shell about ½ inch thick, with the other end left intact. Stuff the potatoes with the selected filling and arrange them upright in a greased baking dish. Cover the tops with tomato slices and add enough water or selected sauce to just reach the tops of the potatoes. Bake in a preheated oven at 400° F for 35 minutes or longer, until the potatoes are tender.

STUFFED ARTICHOKES

Allow 2 globe artichokes per person for a main meal, and 1 per person for appetizers.

globe artichokes   *¾ cup water*
selected filling (see preceding recipes)   *juice of 1 lemon*
1 tablespoon vegetable oil   *salt and black pepper*

Remove the outer, coarse leaves of the artichokes, leaving only the inner, tender ones. Trim these leaves with scissors to a height of about 2 inches Remove the fuzzy choke with a spoon or fork to reveal the heart, and cut away any thorny inner leaves. Trim off the bottoms of the artichokes. Store the prepared artichokes in a bowl of water, to which a squeeze of lemon juice has been added, until they are all ready. Stuff the hearts with a selected filling and place the artichokes in a large pan. Mix the oil, water and lemon juice and season to taste with salt and pepper. Pour this into the pan, bring the liquid to the boil, reduce the heat, cover, and simmer for 1 hour or until the artichokes are tender. Add more water if necessary.

STUFFED APPLES

Serves 4

> 4 large cooking apples, washed   selected filling (see preceding recipes)
> 4 cloves   4 tablespoons butter

Preheat the oven to 350° F. Cut the tops off the apples and reserve them. Core the apples without cutting right through the fruit. Pack with selected filling and stick a clove in the top of each. Put them in a buttered casserole dish, put back the tops, and add a dab of butter to each. Cover and bake for 45 minutes or until the apples and filling are tender.

STUFFED FENNEL

Serves 4

> 4 large fennel bulbs, hard bases cut off,   salt
>   washed   2 cups water or tomato sauce

Put the fennel in a pan of salted boiling water for 10 minutes, drain, cool, and cut in half lengthwise. Preheat the oven to 375° F. Place half the fennel, cut side uppermost, in a casserole dish and pile filling on the top. Carefully put the remaining fennel halves on top. Add the water or tomato sauce and bake for 30 minutes. Serve.

Stuffed Vine Leaves, Cabbage, and Swiss Chard

Methods for filling these leafy vegetables have been given on previous pages. The fillings given at the start of this chapter may be substituted for those given in the previous recipes: Vine Leaves, see page 23; Cabbage Leaves, see page 24; Swiss Chard, see page 25.

Desserts and Sweet Pastries

Whole-wheat Dessert
Semolina Pudding
Almond Rice Pudding
Sweet Pancakes
Fresh Dates
Rose-Flavored Apples
Apples Cooked in Syrup
Fruit Salad
Dried Fruit Salad
Sugared Orange Peel

Sweet Rice-Stuffed Apples
Arabian Doughnuts with
  Syrup
Semolina Cake
Yogurt Cake
Date and Nut Sweets
Almond Cookies
Walnut Treasures
Baklava
Kadayif

The Arab world is famous for its collective sweet tooth and for the desserts and pastries it makes to satisfy this passion. The heat certainly generates a craving for sugar, and in the Middle East I can drink tea or coffee with more sugar than I'd dream of having at home.

Sweet pastries, usually variations of baklava (*baklawa* in Arabic) or kadayif (*konafa* in Arabic), the most famous Middle Eastern pastries, are served on any occasion and they are sold form pastry shops as numerous as our candy stores. Baklava are made froma paper-thin pastry called fila. Kadayif are made from a wheat-flour shredded dough. Both pastries are stuffed with either a nut or cheese filling, baked and then soaked in a very sweet, lemony syrup.

Puddings are normally milky, such as rice or semolina pudding, and served chilled and dusted with cinnamon. Chilled fruit salads made from fresh and dried fruits are favorites to end a meal. Cakes, again soaked in syrup, deep-fried doughnuts, and cookies are eaten as snacks with very strong black coffee.

DESSERTS

WHOLE-WHEAT DESSERT
(Amah)
FERTILE CRESCENT

Serves 4 to 6

This wholesome dessert if prepared at times of celebration such as weddings or the birth of a child. It is filling and can be served as a meal in itself, for, say, a child's birthday party, where both goodness and sweetness are needed.

1 pound whole-wheat berries (sometimes just called whole wheat)
1 teaspoon coriander seeds, washed
1 teaspoon caraway seeds

1⅓ cups sugar
juice of ½ lemon
2 tablespoons rose water (optional)
chopped nuts

Put the whole-wheat berries, coriander, and caraway seeds in a pan, cover with water, and boil until the wheat is tender, about 1 hour (the wheat never gets as soft as rice, but the skins start to open when it is cooked). Drain and transfer to a serving bowl. Put ¾ cup water in a pan, add the sugar and lemon juice, and bring to the boil while stirring. Reduce the heat and simmer until the syrup becomes thick, about 10–12 minutes. Stir in the rose water if used and pour the mixture over the wheat. Cool and garnish with chopped nuts.

SEMOLINA PUDDING
(Mamounia)
SYRIA

Serves 4

In Syria, semolina pudding is eaten for breakfast, dusted with cinnamon powder. It does, however, make a nice dessert and is usually a favorite with children.

4 tablespoons butter
½ cup semolina
⅔ cup sugar
1 cup milk

cinnamon
rose water
chopped almonds

Melt the butter in a heavy pan. Stir in the semolina and cook, while stirring, over low heat for 5 minutes or until lightly browned. Combine the sugar, 1 cup water, and milk in another pan and bring to the boil, while stirring. Slowly stir this into the semolina and cook over a low heat until the mixture thickens to a creamy consistency. If it becomes too thick add a little more water or milk. Spoon the pudding into individual serving bowls and leave to cool. Sprinkle cinnamon, rose water, and chopped almonds over each bowl. Transfer them to a refrigerator and chill before serving.

ALMOND RICE PUDDING
(Mahallabiyya)

Serves 4

¼ cup ground rice (rice flour)	½ teaspoon ground cinnamon
2½ cups milk	¼ teaspoon ground ginger (optional)
⅔ cup sugar	rose water
1 cup ground almonds	chopped nuts

Cream the ground rice with a little of the milk and bring the remainder of the milk to the boil. Stir into the milk the sugar, ground almonds, cinnamon, ginger, and creamed rice. Cook, while stirring, over low heat for 5 minutes, allowing the mixture to very gently boil. Pour it into individual serving bowls and leave to cool. Sprinkle rose water and chopped nuts over each bowl. Transfer them to the refrigerator and chill before serving.

SWEET PANCAKES
(Ataif)

Ataif are thin pancakes akin to the French crêpes, but smaller in diameter. They are made from both yeasted and unyeasted batter. Recipes for both are given here. The traditional filling is a type of clotted cream made from buffaloes' milk. Whipped cream or clotted cream is a fine substitute. Other suggestions for fillings are also given.

YEASTED WATER BATTER

Makes 15 to 20 pancakes

1 teaspoon dried yeast	2¼ cups plain flour, sifted
½ teaspoon sugar	¼ teaspoon salt
1½ cups lukewarm water	

Put the yeast, sugar, and little of the water in a bowl and whisk with a fork. Set aside in a warm place until it starts to bubble and then combine it with the remaining water. Sift the flour and salt into a mixing bowl and form a well in the center. Slowly pour in the yeast mixture and whisk to a smooth batter. Cover and set aside for 1 hour, by which time the batter should be bubbling and risen.

UNYEASTED MILK BATTER

Makes 15 to 20 pancakes

2 cups plain flour, sifted
2 teaspoons sugar
2 eggs, lightly beaten

2 tablespoons melted butter
1 tablespoons rose water (optional)
1½ cups milk

In a blender or mixing bowl combine all the ingredients and beat into a smooth batter. Set aside in the refrigerator for 1 hour.

To Cook the Pancakes   Barely cover the bottom of a heavy frying pan, of about 6 inches diameter, with oil, and heat until the oil is hot but not smoking. Spoon in a small quantity of batter (1–2 tablespoons) and tilt the pan to just coat the bottom completely with batter. Cook until the edges start to brown, then turn the pancake over and brown the other side. Stack the cooked pancakes on a plate in a warm oven. Stuff with a selected filling before serving.

FILLINGS FOR PANCAKES

whipped cream
chopped nuts
chopped nuts mixed with a little sugar
   and cinnamon

cream cheese sweetened with a little
honey

DEEP-FRIED PANCAKES

After filling the pancakes, roll them up so that the edges are tucked in and then deep fry them in hot oil. Drain on paper towels, sprinkle with sugar, honey, and/or lemon juice, and serve.

FRESH DATES
(Tamar)

Fresh dates are delicious and of course very different from the dried sort. There are many different varieties, and a connoisseur can even tell you where a particular type has been grown. Algerian dates are particularly good. They are best served simply on their own.

ROSE-FLAVORED APPLES
SYRIA AND LEBANON

Serves 4

This dessert is refreshing and cooling on a hot summer's day.

1 pound eating apples, cored	*2 tablespoons rose water*
juice of 1 lemon	*cinnamon*
⅓ cup superfine sugar	*crushed ice*

Grate the apples into a mixing bowl. Stir in the lemon juice, sugar, and rose water. Transfer to individual serving bowls, dust with a little cinnamon, and top with crushed ice.

APPLES COOKED IN SYRUP
LEBANON

Serves 4

16 cloves	*1 cup sugar*
4 large eating apples, cored	*whipped cream* or *clotted cream*

Stick 4 cloves into the stalk end of each apple. Put the sugar and ¾ cup water into a pan of the right size to hold the 4 apples upright and bring to the boil. Stir until the sugar dissolves. Place the apples stalk side up in the pan and baste with the syrup. Reduce the heat, cover, and simmer for 12 minutes or until the apples are only just tender. Set the pan with the apples aside to cool. Put the apples into serving bowls, spoon with syrup, and top with cream.

FRUIT SALAD
(Salafet Faowakeh)

Prepare a mixture of any fruit in season; stir in plain yogurt and orange blossom or rose water to taste. Chill, and serve sprinkled with toasted almonds or pine nuts.

DRIED FRUIT SALAD
(Khoshaf)
NORTH AFRICA

Serves 4

> 1 pound dried fruit, e.g. apricots, prunes, raisins, figs, etc., washed
> ⅔ cup sugar (or less)
>
> 1 cup chopped nuts
> juice of 1 lemon

Put all ingredients in a bowl, cover with water, and mix well. Cover the bowl and chill for 24 hours or longer.

SUGARED ORANGE PEEL
(Murabba Tringe)
FERTILE CRESCENT

This method may also be used with lemon and grapefruit peel.

4 large thick-skinned oranges
2¼ cups granulated sugar
confectioners' sugar

Quarter the oranges and remove the peel from the skin. Try to leave the white pith attached to the peel. The flesh is not needed, but you could use it in a fruit salad. Cut the peel into ½-inch wide strips. Put the strips into a pan, cover with 1 cup water, and gently simmer for 20 minutes. Drain and discard the water. Repeat once more.

Put the granulated sugar and water in a heavy pan and gently boil for 30 minutes or until the syrup threads on the end of a spoon. Add the peel and very gently simmer for 1 hour. Now drain the peel strips well and roll them in confectioners' sugar. Allow them to dry on a cake rack and store in an airtight container. Alternatively ladle the peel and syrup into sterilized jars, allow to cool, seal, and store in a dark cold place.

SWEET RICE-STUFFED APPLES
(Tiffah-Bil-Furen)
FERTILE CRESCENT

Serves 4

4 large baking apples	*2 cups cooked rice*
⅔ cup sugar	*4 tablespoons butter, melted*
½ cup raisins, plumped up in hot water	*1 teaspoon cinnamon*

Preheat the oven to 350° F. Cut the tops off the apples and scoop out quite a lot of the centers, using an apple corer or knife. Do not cut through the apple at the bottom end. Sprinkle the insides with a little sugar. Reserve a little of the remaining sugar and combine the rest with the raisins, rice, melted butter, and cinnamon. Pack this filling into the apples and place them in a baking dish. Sprinkle the remaining sugar over them and add water to come a third of the way up the sides of the apples. Put the tops back on the apples and bake for 35–40 minutes in a preheated oven. Baste them occasionally with the cooking water. Serve hot or cold.

ARABIAN DOUGHNUTS WITH SYRUP
(Yo-Yo)

Makes 8 doughnuts

2 medium eggs
2 tablespoons vegetable oil
2 tablespoons orange blossom water
grated rind of 1 small orange
about 1½ cups plain flour

2 teaspoons baking soda
2¼ cups sugar
juice of 1 lemon
oil for deep frying

In a mixing bowl whisk the eggs, oil, orange blossom water, and orange rind into a smooth liquid. Sift together the flour and soda and slowly beat the mixture into the liquid. The dough should become thick enough to only just pour from a spoon. Add more flour if necessary. Cover and set aside in a warm place for 30 minutes, and prepare the syrup. Over a medium heat dissolve the sugar in 1½ cups water, add the lemon juice, and bring to the boil. Reduce heat and gently boil the syrup for 10 minutes.

Heat the oil for deep frying, flour your hands, and form the dough into small-tomato-size balls, flatten them slightly and then push a finger through the center to form a hole. Prepare 3 at a time and deep fry them, turning, until golden brown, about 4–5 minutes. Drain on paper towels and repeat for the remaining dough. Dip them into the syrup and serve. Alternatively pour the syrup over them and leave them for 1 hour to allow it to soak in.

SEMOLINA CAKE
(Basbousa)
EGYPT

½ cup unsalted butter, melted
1 cup superfine sugar
2 small eggs
2 cups fine yellow semolina

1 teaspoon baking powder
½ teaspoon baking soda
blanched split almonds
syrup as for doughnuts above

Cream the butter and the sugar and then beat in the eggs. Stir in ½ cup water. Sift together the semolina, baking powder, and soda, and stir into the butter mixture to form a smooth batter. Preheat the oven to 350° F. Lightly grease an 8-by-12-inch cake pan and pour in the batter. Spread it evenly with the back of a spoon and then score across the top of the cake parallel lines going from the bottom left corner to top right and vice versa, to form diamond shapes. Place an almond in the center of each diamond. Bake in the preheated oven for 35–40 minutes, when the cake should be firm and lightly browned. Prepare the syrup as described in the recipe above and pour it, spoonfuls at a time, over the hot cake. Stop when the cake will not absorb any more and set the cake aside to cool before serving.

YOGURT CAKE
FERTILE CRESCENT

This is a very filling and quite heavy cake. A thin yogurt, or half yogurt and half milk, produces a lighter cake. Serve it on its own or with whipped or clotted cream.

2 cups yogurt	1 teaspoon baking powder
2 beaten eggs	½ teaspoon baking soda
2 cups flour	¼ teaspoon salt
1 cup sugar	**Syrup**
	1¼ cups sugar
	juice of 1 lemon

Preheat the oven to 350° F. In a mixing bowl whisk the yogurt into the beaten eggs. Gradually beat in the flour, 1 cup sugar, baking powder, soda, and salt. Mix well, pour the cake mixture into a greased cake pan, and bake in the preheated oven for 1 hour. Meanwhile make the syrup: dissolve the sugar in ¾ cup water over medium heat, add the lemon juice, bring it to the boil, reduce the heat, and gently boil for 10 minutes. Remove from the heat, cover, and keep warm.

Remove the cake from the oven. Pour the syrup over the cake in the pan. Leave to cool. Remove the cake from the pan and serve.

DATE AND NUT SWEETS
SYRIA

Serves 6 as dessert

These are very sweet and filling, but two or three with coffee at the end of a meal are a great treat for the sweet-toothed.

  1 cup almonds, blanched and chopped
  1 cup walnuts or hazelnuts, chopped

  1 cup dates, fresh or dried, finely
    chopped
  confectioners' sugar

Combine the almonds, walnuts or hazelnuts, and dates and mix them together as best you can (the dates get very sticky). Dust a work surface and rolling pin with confectioners' sugar and roll out the mixture into an approximate square ½ inch thick. Cut this into 1-inch squares and roll the squares in sugar. Arrange the sweets on a plate and serve.

ALMOND COOKIES
(Ghorayebah)
SYRIA

Makes about 40 cookies

  1 cup butter, softened
  3½ cups plain flour
  3 cups confectioners' sugar

  ½ teaspoon almond extract
  40 whole blanched almonds

Cream the butter and sift together the flour and sugar. Fold the mixture into the butter and stir in the almond extract. Knead gently and set to chill in the refrigerator for 30 minutes. Pinch off lumps of dough about 1 inch in diameter and roll them into balls. Flatten them slightly and press a whole almond into the top of each one. Preheat the oven to 350° F and bake the cookies on an ungreased baking sheet for 15 minutes or until they just start to color golden. Cool and then store in an airtight container.

VARIATION: Up to half the flour may be replaced by ground almonds.

WALNUT TREASURES
(Manalsama)
LEBANON

Makes about 20

These are small pastries with a walnut filling buried in the middle.

¾ cup butter, softened
3½ cups plain flour
1 cup superfine sugar

3 tablespoons water or rose water
2 cups walnuts, coarsely ground

Cream the butter. Sift together the flour and ⅓ cup sugar and fold them into the butter. Stir in the water or rose water and knead gently to form a smooth dough. Set aside in the refrigerator for 30 minutes. Combine the ground walnuts with the remaining sugar. Preheat the oven to 350° F. Pinch off lumps of dough about 1 inch in diameter, flatten them in your hand, and put on a teaspoonful of the nut mixture. Fold the pastry around the filling and roll it into a ball. Flatten them slightly and place on an ungreased baking sheet. Decorate the tops with the tines of a fork and bake in the preheated oven for 30 minutes or until they just start to color golden. Cool and store in an airtight container.

SWEET PASTRIES

The perennial pastry favorites in Arab cooking are baklava and kadayif. Baklava is made from layers of buttered fila pastry, with a nut or cheese filling, baked or deep fried and then covered in a sweet lemon-flavored syrup. Kadayif is made from a flour and water dough formed into vermicelli-like strands which are then buttered, layered in a baking dish with a nut or cheese stuffing, baked, and then coated in syrup. Shredded wheat is a fair substitute for kadayif pastry. In my book *Middle Eastern Vegetarian Cookery* I gave basic instructions for preparing baklava and kadayif which I found easy to follow, and I am going to give the same procedure here, but with slightly altered recipes for the fillings. For details on handling fila pastry see page xxi.

The Arabic names for these pastries are *baklawa* and *konafa*, but for consistency, and because baklava and kadayif are the better-known names, I have used them in this book.

The recipes are given in four sections. The first gives a variety of fillings that may be used to fill either baklava or kadayif pastries, the second the preparation of the syrup in which the cooked pastries are soaked, the third the making of baklava, and the fourth the making of kadayif. The amounts used in the recipes are sufficient for 1 pound fila pastry or 1 pound kadayif pastry (or 12 squares of shredded wheat).

FILLINGS FOR BAKLAVA AND KADAYIF

ALMOND AND SESAME SEED FILLING

1½ cups blanched almonds, coarsely ground
1½ cups sesame seeds, browned in 2 tablespoons butter

⅓ cup sugar
1 teaspoon cinnamon
¼ teaspoon nutmeg
2 teaspoons grated lemon rind

Combine the ingredients and mix well.

NUT FILLING

2 egg whites
⅔ cup superfine sugar
4 cups mixed ground nuts (walnuts, almonds, pistachios, hazelnuts, cashew nuts, etc.)

1 teaspoon cinnamon

Beat the egg whites stiff, slowly beat in the sugar, and then fold in the nuts and cinnamon.

CHEESE FILLING

1 pound ricotta cheese or soft cream cheese
2 teaspoons grated lemon peel
sugar to taste

cinnamon to taste
raisins, presoaked and drained (optional)

Beat the cheese to a smooth paste and fold in the lemon peel. Add sugar and cinnamon. Add raisins if you wish.

FRUIT AND ALMOND FILLING

1 pound dried fruit, finely chopped
½ cup fruit preserves or jam

½ cup blanched almonds, chopped
cinnamon to taste

Combine the ingredients and mix well.

SYRUP FOR BAKLAVA

2 cups sugar (up to 2½ cups may be
used for sweeter syrups)
juice of 1 lemon

1 tablespoon orange blossom water or
rose water

Dissolve the sugar in 1 cup water and lemon juice in a pan. Bring the mixture to the boil and simmer for 10–15 minutes or until it is slightly viscous. Stir in the orange blossom water or rose water and remove from the heat.

The syrup should be cooled or even slightly chilled, and then poured over the hot pastries as soon as they come out of the oven.

MAKING BAKLAVA

I · DIAMOND PASTRIES

Makes 30 to 40 pastries

1 pound fila pastry dough
1 cup unsalted butter, melted

selected filling (see above)
syrup (see above)

Choose a large, not too deep, baking tin or dish (e.g. 12 by 16 inches). Brush half the pastry sheets and the baking pan sides and bottom with melted butter. Fit the sheets into the bottom of the pan one at a time, folding to fit as necessary. Spread the prepared filling over the top in a ½–¾-inch layer. Brush the remaining sheets of pastry with melted butter and place them one at a time on top of the filling. Again fold to fit as necessary. If there is any butter left pour it over the top layer. With a very sharp knife cut through all the layers diagonally to form diamond shapes. Bake them in a preheated oven at 375° F for 30 minutes and then at 450° F for 15 minutes. The baklava should be nicely browned. Remove from the oven and immediately pour the cold or chilled syrup over them. Allow to cool before serving.

Alternatively, for very moist baklava, pour two-thirds of the syrup over the hot baklava, allow them to cool, and then pour the remaining syrup over them.

VARIATION: Some people prefer to omit the syrup and serve the baklava crisp and sprinkled with a little confectioners' sugar.

II · CIGAR PASTRIES

Makes 30 to 40 pastries

Take 2–3 sheets of fila pastry dough and brush them with melted butter. Lay one sheet on top of the other and place 4–5 tablespoons of selected filling along the long side of the top sheet. Roll it all up like a piece of carpet and place the roll in a buttered dish. Cut the roll to fit the dish if necessary. Repeat until all the fila dough and filling have been used up and pack the rolls close together in the dish. Brush them with melted butter and then cut them diagonally into 2–3-inch lengths. Bake the baklava at 350° F until nicely browned. Remove them from the oven and pour cold syrup over them. Allow the baklava to cool before serving. Alternatively, cut the rolls into 2-inch lengths and deep fry them in hot oil until golden brown (2–3 minutes). Drain and dip in cold syrup.

III · FINGER PASTRIES

Makes 40 to 50 pastries

Preheat the oven to 375° F. Cut the sheets of fila pastry into 10-by-6-inch rectangles. Brush each with melted butter and spread along the narrow side a heaped teaspoonful of filling. Roll the fila into a finger shape and place on a buttered baking sheet. Repeat for all the pastry and filling. Bake for 20 minutes or until nicely browned. Remove from the oven and pour syrup over them while still hot. Drain and transfer to a serving dish. Serve when cool.

Filled with an almond or pistachio nut filling, these pastries are known as bride's fingers (*asabeh-el-aruss*).

MAKING KADAYIF

1 pound kadayif dough or 12
   shredded wheat
1 cup unsalted butter, melted

selected filling (see above)
syrup (see above)

Remove any lumps from the kadayif dough by gently separating the strands with your fingers. Place half the dough in a buttered, not too deep, large square or round baking dish (e.g. 12 by 16 inches) and brush with butter. Alternatively, if using shredded wheat, break up half the shredded wheat and lay the shreds in the buttered dish and brush with butter. Now evenly spread the filling over the dough or shredded wheat, cover evenly with the remaining dough or shredded wheat, and brush generously with butter. Bake the kadayif in a preheated oven at 375° F for 45 minutes or until golden. Remove it from the oven and pour the cold syrup over it. Cool and cut the kadayif into small squares.

INDIVIDUAL KADAYIF

Using a sharp knife hollow out the center of shredded wheat biscuits and stuff them with a selected filling (see above). Brush generously with melted butter. Bake the filled shredded wheat in a preheated oven at 375° F for 30 minutes and then pour cold syrup over them.

NOTE: The shredded wheat is possibly easier to handle for stuffing if soaked in milk for 5 minutes and then drained.

Drinks

Arab Coffee
Mint Tea
Yogurt Drink
  (Aryaan or Laban)

Coffee is an essential element in Arabic social life and one which allows the Arab to express his great hospitality. Coffee, always made by the same ritual, is offered to guests as a formality, and they are expected to join in the ritual by accepting two or three small cups. The Koran forbids the drinking of alcohol, and coffee plays the same role as a drink may do in the West. The original name in Arabic for coffee was in fact the same as for wine, *kahwah*. Coffee is drunk many times in a day. It is made very strong, but because of the boiling procedure used in the preparation, the caffeine content is usually low.

Tea is also popular but to a lesser extent. It is served very sweet, often flavored with mint or made solely from mint leaves. Water flavored with orange blossom or rose water or sweetened with sugar-cane juice, a salty yogurt drink called *aryaan*, or *laban*, and tea are drinks sold in the streets by vendors. If alcohol is available it is usually as beer or in the form of anise-flavored spirits called arak or *raki*, similar to pastis.

ARABIC COFFEE

The coffee beans are roasted in an iron ladle and then ground very fine in a brass pestle and mortar called a *tahrini*. The ground coffee is boiled in a long-handled coffee pot, a *rakwi*, with sugar and water, and served in very small cups without handles. The coffee is flavored with cardamom pods and served sweet (*mazboutah*) or very sweet (*hilweh*). Unsweetened coffee (*murrah*) is not that popular. Two different methods for boiling the coffee are common. The second method, in which the coffee is brought to the boil three times, is the Bedouin method.

METHOD I

4 small coffee cups cold water
4 heaped teaspoons coarsely ground
  espresso-roasted coffee

2 split pods cardamom
sugar

Put the water, coffee, and split cardamom pods in a long-handled coffee pot or small saucepan and bring to the boil. Reduce the heat and leave to simmer for 20 minutes. Serve in a very small cup one-third full, and sweeten to taste.

METHOD II

ingredients as above

Put the water in the pot or saucepan, add the cardamom pods, and bring to the boil. Remove from the heat and add the coffee and sugar to taste. Stir, then reheat until the coffee foams and rises. Remove from the heat. Repeat the process until the coffee stops foaming and rising and just boils. Serve in very small coffee cups one-third full.

VARIATION: Add 1 teaspoon of ground ginger to the coffee pot along with the coffee.

MINT TEA

Serves 4

3 teaspoons green China tea
2 tablespoons sugar (more or less to
  your taste)

3 tablespoons freshly chopped mint
boiling water

Put the tea, sugar, and mint in a teapot. Fill with boiling water and leave to brew for 4–5 minutes. Stir, allow to settle, and then pour the tea into serving glasses or cups. Alternatively, drain the tea from the pot, chill, and serve cold.

YOGURT DRINK
(*Aryaan* or *Laban*)

Makes 5 cups

> 2½ *cups plain yogurt*
> *salt*
> *chopped fresh mint*

In either a bowl or a blender, beat the yogurt and 2½ cups water together.
Salt to taste, and chill. Serve garnished with mint.

INDEX

acorn squash, stuffed, 159
adas be sabanigh (lentils and spinach), 146
adas biz-ruz (rice and lentil soup), 39
Algerian eggplant salad (*batenjal m'char-mel*), 71–72
almond(s)
  chicken with, yellow, 117
  cookies (*ghorayebah*), 174
  and fruit filling for baklava and kadayif, 177
  rice pudding (*mahallabiyya*), 167
  soup (*shorabat loz*), 35–36
amah (whole-wheat dessert), 165–66
anchovy fingers, 9–10
appetizers, *see* mezze
apple(s)
  beanpot, Arabian, 147–48
  cooked in syrup, 169–70
  fried, pepper and tomato salad with, 74–75
  rose-flavored, 169
  stuffed, 162
  sweet rice-stuffed (*tiffah-bil-furen*), 171
apricot and lamb *tagine*, 98
Arab fish soup, 46–47
Arabian apple beanpot, 147–48
Arabian doughnuts with syrup (*yo-yo*), 172
Arabian meat pizza (*lahma bi-ajeen*), 54
Arabian omelet (*eggah*), 31–32
Arabic coffee, 183–84
Arab lamb stew (*yakni*), 105–6
artichoke(s)
  hearts, in oil, 21–22
  stuffed, 161
aryaan (yogurt drink), 185
ataif (sweet pancakes), 167–68

baba ghanooj (eggplant purée)
  without tahini, 14
  with tahini, 15
Baghdad chicken and rice, 126
baklava, 175
  almond and sesame seed filling for, 176
  cheese filling for, 176
  fruit and almond filling for, 177
  making, 177–78
  nut filling for, 176
  syrup for, 177

bamia (ground meat with okra), 100–1
barbecued fish (*samak meshwi*), 88–89
  kebabs (*samek kebab*), 89
basbousa (semolina cake), 172–73
bazargan (spiced burghul wheat salad), 75
bean(s), 129
  apple beanpot, Arabian, 147–48
  broad brown, see *ful medames*
  broad white, see *ful nabed*
  buying and cooking, xxiii
  casserole, fresh (*tajine ful*), 149
  falafel, 18–19
  fava (broad), rice with (*roz ou ful*), 133
  lamb with rice and, 113
  and spinach salad, 77
beef, 97
  chicken stuffed with, 123
  couscous with, 145
  meatball soup (*kufta* soup), 44
    chicken stock and, 45
    lamb stock and, 45
  pizza, Arabian (*lahma bi-ajeen*), 54
  and rice, Yemeni, 114
  shish kebabs, 28
  stew, with eggs, Egyptian (*dfeena*), 106
brain(s), lamb
  fried, 29–30
  salad with dressing, 29
bread
  pita, *see* pita bread
  quick spiced onion (*khoubiz basali*), 57
  toasted, and salad (*fattoush*), 68
  unyeasted Arab (*khobz*), 57–58
bread dips, *see* dip
brik (fried egg pastries), 58–59
burghul wheat (bulgur or cracked wheat), xxv–xxvi, 129, 136
  dry roasting method for cooking, 136
  and eggplant pilav, 137
  fish and (fish *kibbi*), 92–93
  frying method for cooking, 136–37
  and lamb
    cakes, 26
    stew, 138
  salad (*tabbouleh*), 30–31
    spiced, (*bazargan*), 75
butter, clarified (*samneh*), xxi

butter beans, in Arabian apple beanpot, 147–48
butternut squash, stuffed, 159

cabbage leaves, stuffed, 24
cake
  semolina (basbousa), 172–73
  yogurt, 173
calf kidneys and liver casserole, 115
calf livers
  with garlic, skewered, 114–15
  and kidney casserole, 115
carrot salad, Moroccan orange and, 70
casserole
  fish
    and chick-pea, 90
    and lamb, 91
  fresh bean (tajine ful), 149
  lamb with chick-pea, spiced, 147
  liver and kidney, 115
  pilav rice and fish, 90–91
  rice with lamb (roz tajin), 112–13
cheddar, grilled, 10–11
cheese
  feta, cucumber with (michoteta), 7
  filling
    for baklava and kadayif, 176
    for pastries, 62
  fried, 11
  grilled, 10–11
  pastries, lamb and, 59–60
  yogurt (labna), xix–xx
chicken, 116–26
  with almonds, yellow, 117
  and apricot tagine (with or instead of lamb), 98
  with chick-peas, 118–19
  couscous with, 145
  curried roasted, 120–21
  Egyptian green herb soup with (melokhia), 42–43
  fried, with spinach, 124
  grilled (farareej mashwi), 117–18
  harira (soup) with lamb and, 40–41
  honey roasted, 120
  with lemon juice, hot spiced, 116
  meatballs, 26–27
  meat-stuffed, 123
  with olives, 119
  pastries, 60
  and rice
    and orange pilav, 125–26
    Baghdad, 126
  spicy stuffed, Moroccan style, 122–23
  stock
    and meatball soup, 45

  for Egyptian green herb soup (melokhia), 42
  stuffed with rice, roast (dajaj mahshi), 121–22
  tagine, 124–25
chick-pea(s), 6
  chicken with, 118–19
  falafel, 18–19
  and fish casserole, 90
  harira (soup), 41–42
  and lamb casserole, spiced, 147
  and mixed nuts, 11–12
  roasted, 6
  soup, 36
  and tahini dip (hummus bi tahini), 15–16
chopping, methods of, xxv
cigar pastries, 178
clarified butter (samneh), xxi
coffee, Arabic, 183–84
cookies, almond (ghorayebah), 174
couscous, 129, 142
  basic steps in the preparation of, 142
  to make, 144–45
    grains of, 143
  with sweet Moroccan sauce, 145–46
couscousier, 142
cracked wheat, see burghul wheat
croquettes
  bean (falafel), 18–19
  meat (kofta), 101–2
cucumber
  with feta cheese (michoteta), 7
  with yogurt, 8
cumin and tahini dip, 12

dajaj mahshi (roast chicken stuffed with rice), 121–22
date(s)
  fresh (tamar), 169
  lamb with, 107
  and nut sweets, 174
  and orange salad, Moroccan, 74
  stuffed (tamar al gibna), 7
desserts, 163–75
  almond cookies (ghorayebah), 174
  almond rice pudding (mahallabiyya), 167
  apples cooked in syrup, 169–70
  date(s)
    fresh (tamar), 169
    and nut sweets, 174
  doughnuts with syrup, Arabian (yo-yo), 172
  dried fruit (khoshaf), 170
  fruit salad (salafet faowakeh), 170
  orange peel, sugared (murabba tringe), 170–71

pancakes, sweet (*ataif*), 167–68
rice-stuffed apples, sweet (*tiffah-bil-fu-ren*), 171
rose-flavored apples, 169
semolina cake (*basbousa*), 172–73
semolina pudding (*mamounia*), 166
walnut treasures (*manalsama*), 175
whole-wheat (*amah*), 165–66
yogurt cake, 173
diamond pastries, 177–78
dip
  baba ghanooj (eggplant purée)
    without tahini, 14
    with tahini, 15
  eggplant, spiced, 13
  hummus bi tahini (chick-pea and tahini), 15–16
  tahini and cumin, 12
  zahtar (seed and nut), 12–13
dolmas, 22–25
doughnuts with syrup, Arabian (*yo-yo*), 172
dressing, salad, *see* salad dressing
dried fruit(s)
  and almond filling, for baklava and kadayif, 177
  and rice filling, for *mishshi*, 155
  salad (*khoshaf*), 170
drink(s), 181–85
  coffee, 183–84
  mint tea, 184
  yogurt (*aryaan* or *laban*), 185

egg(s)
  Arabian omelet (*eggah*), 31–32
  beef stew with, Egyptian (*dfeena*), 106
  in a lamb coat, 102
  and lemon soup, 40
  pastries, fried (*brik*), 58–59
eggah (Arabian omelet), 31–32
eggplant(s)
  and burghul wheat pilav, 137
  dip, spiced, 13
  lamb and, baked, 109
  in lamb and vegetables, baked, 108–9
  lamb with rice and, 111–12
  preparation for cooking, xxiii–xxiv
  purée (*baba ghanooj*)
    without tahini, 14
    with tahini, 15
  salad
    Algerian (*batenjal m'charmel*), 71–72
    Lebanese, 71
  stuffed, 158
Egyptian beef stew with eggs, 106

Egyptian fish plaki, 92
Egyptian green herb soup (*melokhia*), 42–43

falafel, 18–19
  hot sauce for, 20
  relish for, 20
farareej mashwi (grilled chicken), 117–18
fava (broad) beans
  in Arabian apple beanpot, 147–48
  rice with (*roz ou ful*), 133
fennel, stuffed, 162
feta cheese, cucumber with (*michoteta*), 7
fila pastry (*ajeen*), xxi–xxii
finger pastries, 178
fish, 79–93
  anchovy or sardine fingers, 9–10
  baked
    and burghul wheat (fish *kibbi*), 92–93
    Egyptian fish plaki, 92
    with hot chili and tahini sauce, 83
    with nut stuffing, 85
    with tahini sauce, 82–83
    with taratoor sauce, 84–85
  barbecued (*samak meshwi*), 88–89
    kebabs (*samek kebab*), 89
  and burghul wheat (fish *kibbi*), 92–93
  and chick-pea casserole, 90
  couscous with, 145
  fried
    spicy, 10
    in spicy zucchini and tomato sauce, 87
    in tomato sauce, 86–87
    with yellow rice, 87–88
  kebabs, barbecued (*samek kebab*), 89
  and lamb casserole, 91
  and pilav rice casserole, 90–91
  pilav rice to serve with, 81–82
  plaki, Egyptian, 92
  salt or smoked, in tahini sauce, 86
  smoked herring and garlic, 9
  soup, Arab, 46–47
flaky pastries, 60
  cheese filling for, 62
  dough for, 61
  lamb filling for, 62
  preparing, 63
fruit(s)
  dried
    and rice filling for *mishshi*, 155
    salad (*khoshaf*), 170
  salad (*salafet faowakeh*), 170
  see also apple; date; orange
ful medames (broad brown beans), 17

ful nabed (broad white beans), 36
  mezze, 17–18
  soup, 36

garlic
  skewered liver with, 114–15
  and smoked herring, 9
ghorayebah (almond cookies), 174
grains, 129
green bean(s)
  casserole, fresh (*tajine ful*), 149
  in oil, 21
  and potato salad, 69
green herb soup, Egyptian (*melokhia*), 42–43
grinding, methods of, xxv

haloumy cheese, grilled, 10–11
harira (Moroccan soup)
  chick-pea, 41–42
  with lamb and chicken, 40–41
harissa (hot pepper sauce), xxvi
  baked fish with tahini and, 83
harissa (meat and wheat stew), 109–10
herring, smoked, and garlic, 9
honey roasted chicken, 120
hors d'oeuvre, *see* mezze
hot chili sauce, baked fish with tahini and, 83
hubbard squash, stuffed, 159
hummus bi tahini (chick-pea and tahini dip), 15–16

Iraqi steamed rice, 131–32

kadayif, 175
  almond and sesame seed filling for, 176
  cheese filling for, 176
  fruit and almond filling for, 177
  individual, 179
  making, 179
  nut filling for, 176
kebabs
  lamb, 27–28
    marinated, 110
  liver with garlic, 114–15
  shish (ground meat), 28
khobz (unyeasted Arab bread), 57–58
khoubiz-arabi, see pita bread
khoubiz basali (quick spiced onion bread), 57
khoubiz bij-jibin (pizza sandwich), 53
khouzi (whole roast lamb), 103–4

kibbi, 138–39
  baked on a tray (*kibbi bil sanieh*), 141
  basic, 139
  fish (fish and burghul wheat), 92–93
  fried, 140
  raw (*kibbi nayye*), 140
  stuffed (*kibbeyet*), 140
  stuffing, basic, 139
kidney and liver casserole, 115
kishk soup (*shurabat al kishk*), 43–44
kofta (meat croquettes), 101–2
  and vegetable *tagine*, 99–100
koushari (rice, noodles, and lentils with tomato sauce), 135
kufta soup (meatball soup), 44

laban (yogurt drink), 185
  see also yogurt
labna (yogurt cheese), xx–xxi
lamb, 97
  and apricot *tagine*, 98
  with beans and rice, 113
  brain(s)
    fried, 29–30
    salad with dressing, 29
  and burghul wheat
    cakes, 26
    stew, 138
  chicken stuffed with, 123
  and chick-pea casserole, spiced, 147
  couscous with, 144–45
  with cumin, 108
  with dates, 107
  and eggplant, baked, 109
  eggs in a lamb coat, 102
  filling for pastries, 62
  and fish casserole, 91
  kebabs, 27–28
    marinated, 110
  kibbi, see *kibbi*
  with lemon juice, 111
  liver(s)
    and kidney casserole, 115
    with garlic, skewered, 114–15
  pastries, cheese and, 59–60
  patties, 25–26
  pizza, Arabian (*lahma bi-ajeen*), 54
  with prunes, 107
  with rice and eggplant, 111–12
  with rice casserole, 112–13
  and rice filling, for dolmas, 22
  roast, whole (*khouzi*), 103–4
  roasted, Moroccan style, 102
  shish kebabs, 28
  soup
    harira, with chicken, 40–41

lentil and, 38
  meatball (*kufta* soup), 44–45
  Yemeni, 46
stew, Arab (*yakni*), 105–6
stuffed breast of, 104
tagine, Tunisian, 99
tongues with tahini, 30
and vegetables, baked, 108–9
Lebanese eggplant salad, 71
lemon
  and egg soup, 40
  juice
    hot spiced chicken with, 116
  lamb with, 111
lentil(s)
  baked with noodles (*rishta*), 149
  and noodles in butter, 134
  pot, hot, 148
  and rice
    and noodles with tomato sauce (*koushari*), 135
    pilav (*mujaddarah*), 132
    and spinach pilav, 133
  salad, 76
  soup (*shourabat adas*), 37–38
    lamb and, 38
    noodle and (*rishta*), 39–40
    rice and (*adas biz-ruz*), 39
    spinach and (*adas bis-sileq*), 38–39
    tomato and, 38
  and spinach (*adas be sabanigh*), 146
    pilav, rice and, 133
liver(s)
  with garlic, skewered, 114–15
  and kidney casserole, 115

mackerel, spicy fried, 10
muhullubiyyu (almond rice pudding), 167
mamounia (semolina pudding), 166
manalsama (walnut treasures), 175
meat
  croquettes (*kofta*), 101–2
  filling for *mishshi*, 154
    rice and, 154
  ground, 100
    with okra, 100–1
    see also meatball(s)
  pies, open (*sfiha*), 54–55
    vegetable and, 56
  pizza, Arabian (*lahma bi-ajeen*), 54
  and wheat stew (*harissa*), 109–10
  see also beef; lamb; mutton; veal
meatball(s)
  chicken, 26–27
  kofta and vegetable *tagine*, 99–100

soup (*kufta* soup), 44
  chicken stock and, 45
  lamb stock and, 45
melokhia, Egyptian green herb soup, 42–43
mezze (hors d'oeuvre), 3–31
  anchovy or sardine fingers, 9–10
  Arabian omelet (*eggah*), 31–32
  artichoke hearts in oil, 21–22
  cheese
    fried, 11
    grilled, 10–11
  chicken meatballs, 26–27
  chick-peas
    and mixed nuts, 11–12
    roasted, 6
  cucumber
    with feta cheese (*michoteta*), 7
    with yogurt, 8
  dip, *see* dip
  dolmas (stuffed leaves), 22–25
  falafel, 18–19
  fish, spicy fried, 10
  ful medames, 17
  ful nabed, 17–18
  green beans in oil, 21
  lamb
    and burghul wheat cakes, 26
    brains, fried, 29–30
    brain salad with dressing, 29
    kebabs, 27–28
    patties, 25–26
    tongues with tahini, 30
  shish (ground meat) kebabs, 28
  shrimp pâté, 8–9
  simple, 5–6
  smoked herring and garlic, 9
  stuffed cabbage leaves, 24
  stuffed dates (*tamar al gibna*), 7
  stuffed swiss chard, 25
  stuffed vine leaves, 23–24
  tabbouleh (burghul wheat salad), 30–31
  vegetables cooked in oil, 20–22
michoteta (cucumber with feta cheese), 7
mint, yogurt sauce with, xx
mint tea, 184
mishshi (stuffed vegetables), 151–62
  apples, 162
  artichokes, 161
  eggplants, 158
  fennel, 162
  filling(s) for, 153
    meat, 154
    meat and rice, 154
    rice, 154–55
    rice and dried fruit, 155
  garnish for, 157

mishshi (stuffed vegetables), *continued*
  onions, 160
  peppers, red or green, 159
  potatoes, 161
  squash, 159
  stabilized yogurt sauce for, 156–57
  tomatoes, 160
  tomato filling for, 155–56
  tomato sauce for, 156
    quick, 156
  zucchini, 158
mixed salad, 67
Moroccan orange and carrot salad, 70
Moroccan orange and date salad, 74
Moroccan style roasted lamb, 102
Moroccan tomato and pepper salad, 72–73
mraquish biz zatar (seasoned pita bread), 53
mujaddarah (lentil and rice pilav), 132
murabba tringe (sugared orange peel), 170–71
mutton, 97
  meatball soup (*kufta* soup), 44
    chicken stock and, 45
    lamb stock and, 45

noodle(s)
  lentils and, in butter, 134
  lentils baked with (*rishta*), 149
  and lentil soup (*rishta*), 39
  with rice and lentils with tomato sauce (*koushari*), 135
  rice with (*roz bel shaghia*), 134–35
nut(s), xxii–xxiii
  blanching, xxiii
  chick-peas and mixed, 11–12
  chopping, slicing, and grinding, xxiii
  and date sweets, 174
  filling for baklava and kadayif, 176
  pine, xxii–xxiii
  roasting, xxiii
  stuffing, baked fish with, 85
  see also almond; walnut

okra, ground meat with (*bamia*), 100–1
olive(s)
  chicken with, 119
  and orange salad, 74
olive oil
  artichoke hearts in, 21–22
  green beans in, 21
  vegetables cooked in, 20–22
omelet, Arabian (*eggah*), 31–32

onion(s)
  bread, quick spiced (*khoubiz basali*), 57
  salad, orange and, 73
  stuffed, 160
orange
  chicken and rice pilav with, 125–26
  peel, sugared (*murabba tringe*), 170–71
  salad
    carrot and, Moroccan, 70
    date and, Moroccan, 74
    olive and, 74
    onion and, 73
    radish and, 73

pancakes, sweet (*ataif*), 167–68
  deep-fried, 168
  filling for, 168
pasta dishes, 134–35
  see also noodles
pastries
  chicken, 60
  egg, fried (*brik*), 58–59
  fila (*ajeen*), xxi–xxii
  lamb and cheese, 59–60
  shortcrust and flaky, 60
    cheese filling for, 62
    dough for, 61
    lamb filling for, 62
    preparing, 63
    vegetable filling for, 62
  sweet, 175–79
pâté, shrimp, 8–9
pea casserole, fresh (*tajine ful*), 149
peppers, red or green
  stuffed, 159
  and tomato salad
    fried apple and, 74–75
    Moroccan, 72–73
pickled vegetables, 77
pies
  meat and vegetable, open, 56
  triangle spinach (*sbanikh bil-ajn*), 56
  vegetable, open, 55
pilav, 129
  burghul, simple, 137
  burghul wheat and eggplant, 137
  chicken, rice, and orange, 125–26
  lentil, rice, and spinach, 133
  lentil and rice (*mujaddarah*), 132
  rice, 81–82
    and fish casserole, 90–91
pine nuts, xxii–xxiii
pita bread, 51
  Arabian meat pizza using dough for, 54
  basic (*khoubiz-arabi*), 52

open meat pies (*sfiha*) using dough for, 54–55

open vegetable pies using dough for, 55

pizza sandwich (*khoubiz bij-jibin*), using dough for, 53

recipes using dough for, 52–56

seasoned (*mraquish biz zatar*), 53

triangle spinach pies (*sbanikh bil-ajn*), 56

pizza

  meat, Arabian (*lahma bi-ajeen*), 54

  sandwich (*khoubiz bij-jibin*), 53

potato(es)

  salad, 68–69

    green bean and, 69

    spicy potato and caraway seed, 69

  stuffed, 161

prunes, lamb with, 107

pudding

  almond rice (*mahallabiyya*), 167

  semolina (*mamounia*), 166

quick spiced onion bread (*khoubiz basali*), 57

radish salad, orange and, 73

relish, falafel, 20

rice, 129–33

  almond pudding (*mahallabiyya*), 167

  beef and, Yemeni, 114

  chicken and, Baghdad, 126

  and chicken and orange pilav, 125–26

  chicken stuffed with, roast (*dajaj mahshi*), 121–22

  chicken with lemon juice and, hot spiced, 116

  with fava (broad) beans (*roz ou ful*), 133

  filling for *mishshi*, 154–55

    dried fruit and, 155

    meat and, 154

  and ground lamb filling, for dolmas, 22

  Iraqi steamed, 131–32

  lamb with

    casserole, 112–13

    and beans, 113

    and eggplant, 111–12

  and lentil(s)

    pilav (*mujaddarah*), 132

    soup (*adas biz-ruz*), 39

    and spinach pilav, 133

  method I for cooking, 130

  method II for cooking, 130–31

  with noodles

    and lentils with tomato sauce (*koushari*), 135

    roz bel shaghia, 134–35

  pilav, 81–82

    and fish casserole, 90–91

    steamed, Iraqi, 131–32

  -stuffed apples, sweet (*tiffah-bil-furen*), 171

  and vegetable filling, for dolmas, 23

  yellow, 131

    fried fish with, 87–88

rishta (lentils baked with noodles), 149

rishta (noodle and lentil soup), 39–40

rose-flavored apples, 169

roz bel shaghia (rice with noodles), 134–35

roz ou ful (rice with fava beans), 133

roz tajin (rice with lamb casserole), 112–13

salad, 65–77

  burghul wheat, spiced (*bazargan*), 75

  dried fruit (*khoshaf*), 170

  eggplant

    Algerian (*batenjal m'charmel*), 71–72

    Lebanese, 71

  fruit (*salafet faowakeh*), 170

  lamb brain, with dressing, 29

  lentil, 76

  mixed, 67

  orange

    and carrot, Moroccan, 70

    date and, Moroccan, 74

    olive and, 74

    onion and, 73

    radish and, 73

  potato, 68–69

    and caraway seed, spicy, 69

    and green bean, 69

  spinach

    and bean, 77

    and walnut, 76

  tabbouleh (burghul wheat), 30–31

  toasted bread and (*fattoush*), 68

  tomato, 70

    fried apple, pepper, and, 74–75

    pepper and, Moroccan, 72–73

  zucchini, 70–71

salad dressing, xxiv

  lamb brain salad with, 29

salafet faowakeh (fruit salad), 170

salt fish, in tahini sauce, 86

samek kebab (barbecued fish kebabs), 89

sandwich, pizza (*khoubiz bij-jibin*), 53

sardine fingers, 9–10

sauce

  hot, for falafel, 20

sauce, *continued*
  hot chili and tahini, baked fish with, 83
  hot pepper (*harissa*), xxvi, 109–10
  spicy zucchini and tomato, fried fish in, 87
  sweet Moroccan, couscous with, 145–46
  tahini (*taratour bi tahini*), 13–14
    baked fish with, 82–83
    baked fish with hot chili and, 83
    for lamb patties, 25
    lamb tongues with, 30
    salt fish or smoked fish in, 86
  taratoor, baked fish with, 84–85
  tomato
    fried fish in, 86–87
    for *mishshi*, 156
    rice, noodles, and lentils with (*koushari*), 135
    spicy zucchini and, fried fish in, 87
  yogurt
    stabilized, 156–57
    with mint, xx
savory pastries, 58–63
  see also pastries
sbanikh bil-ajn (triangle spinach pies), 56
semolina
  cake (*basbousa*), 172–73
  pudding (*mamounia*), 166
sesame seed and almond filling for baklava and kadayif, 176
sfiha (open meat pies), 54
shish (ground meat) kebabs, 28
shorabat ful nabed (broad bean soup), 36
shorabat loz (almond soup), 35–36
shortcrust pastries, 60
  cheese filling for, 62
  dough for, 61
  lamb filling for, 62
  preparing, 63
shourabat adas (lentil soup), 37–38
shrimp pâté, 8–9
shurabat al kishk (kishk soup), 43–44
shurabat al-mawzat (tomato soup), 36–37
smoked fish, in tahini sauce, 86
smoked herring and garlic, 9
soup, 33–47
  almond (*shorabat loz*), 35–36
  broad bean (*shorabat ful nabed*), 36
  chicken stock and meatball, 45
  chick-pea (*harira*), 41–42
  egg and lemon, 40
  fish, Arab, 46–47
  green herb, Egyptian (*melokhia*), 42–43
  harira with lamb and chicken, 40–41
  kishk (*shurabat al kishk*), 43–44

lamb
  and lentil, 38
  Yemeni, 46
lamb stock and meatball, 45
lentil (*shourabat adas*), 37–38
meatball (*kufta* soup), 44–45
noodle and lentil (*rishta*), 39
rice and lentil (*adas biz-ruz*), 39
spinach and lentil (*adas bis-sileq*), 38–39
tomato (*shurabat al-mawzat*), 36–37
  and lentil, 38
spiced onion bread, quick (*khoubiz basali*), 57
spinach
  fried chicken with, 124
  and lentil(s)
    adas be sabanigh, 146
    and rice pilav, 133
    pies, triangle (*sbanikh bil-ajin*), 56
    salad, walnut and, 76
    soup (*adas bis-sileq*), 38–39
squash, stuffed, 159
stew
  beef, with eggs, Egyptian (*dfeena*), 106
  lamb
    Arab (*yakni*), 105–6
    burghul wheat and, 138
    with dates, 107
    with prunes, 107
  meat and wheat (*harissa*), 109–10
  tagine, 98
    chicken, 124–25
    kofta (meatball) and vegetable, 99–100
    lamb, Tunisian, 99
    lamb and apricot, 98
stock, xxiv
  chicken
    for Egyptian green herb soup (*melokhia*), 42
    and meatball soup, 45
  lamb, and meatball soup, 45
string beans, *see* green beans
sweet pastries, 175–79
  walnut treasures (*manalsama*), 175
  see also baklava; kadayif
sweets, date and nut, 174
swiss chard, stuffed, 25
syrup
  apples cooked in, 169–70
  Arabian doughnuts with (*yo-yo*), 172
  for baklava, 177

ta'amia, 18
  see also falafel
tabbouleh (burghul wheat salad), 30–31

tagine
  chicken, 124–25
  kofta (meatball) and vegetable, 99–100
  lamb and apricot, 98
  lamb, Tunisian, 99
tahini, xxvi
  baba ghanooj (eggplant purée) with, 15
  and chick-pea dip (*hummus bi tahini*), 15
  and cumin, 12
  dip or sauce (*taratour bi tahini*), 13–14
  sauce
    baked fish with, 82–83
    baked fish with hot chili and, 83
    for lamb patties, 25
    lamb tongues with, 30
    salt fish or smoked fish in, 86
tajine ful (fresh bean casserole), 149
tamar (fresh dates), 169
tamar al gibna (stuffed dates), 7
taratoor sauce
  baked fish with, 84–85
taratour bi tahini (tahini dip or sauce), 13–14
tea, mint, 184
tiffah bil furen (sweet rice-stuffed apples), 171
toasted bread and salad (*fattoush*), 68
tomato(es)
  filling for *mishshi*, 155–56
  salad, 70
    fried apple, pepper and, 74–75
    pepper and, Moroccan, 72–73
  sauce
    fried fish in, 86–87
    for *mishshi*, 156
    for *mishshi*, quick, 156
    rice, noodles, and lentil with (*koushari*), 135
    spicy zucchini and, fried fish in, 87
  soup (*shurabat al-mawzat*), 36–37
    lentil and, 38
  stuffed, 160
tongues, lamb, with tahini, 30
triangle spinach pies (*sbanikh bil-ajn*), 56
Tunisian lamb *tagine*, 99

veal
  roasted, Moroccan style, 102
  stuffed breast of, 104

vegetable(s)
  cooked in oil, as mezze, 20–22
  filling for pastries, 62
  and *kofta* (meatball) *tagine*, 99–100
  lamb and, baked, 108–9
  pickled, 77
  pies, open, 55
    meat and, 56
  and rice filling, for dolmas, 23
  stuffed, *see* dolmas; *mishshi*
  see also individual vegetables
vine leaves, xxiv–xxv
  stuffed, 23–24

walnut(s)
  and spinach salad, 76
  treasures (*manalsama*), 175
wheat
  burghul, *see* burghul wheat
  whole-
    dessert (*amah*), 165–66
    and meat stew (*harissa*), 109–10

yakni (Arab lamb stew), 105–6
yellow chicken with almonds, 117
Yemeni beef and rice, 114
Yemeni lamb soup, 46
yogurt (*laban*), xix
  cake, 173
  cheese (*laban*), xx–xxi
  cucumber with, 8
  drink, (*aryaan* or *laban*), 185
  sauce
    with mint, xx
    stabilized, 156–57
yo-yo (Arabian doughnuts with syrup), 172

zahtar, 12–13
  pita bread seasoned with, 53
zucchini
  salad, 70–71
  stuffed, 158
  and tomato sauce, spicy, fried fish in, 87

ABOUT THE AUTHOR

DAVID SCOTT, a well-known cookbook writer in England, is the author of *Middle Eastern Vegetarian Cooking, Recipes for Living, Grains, Beans and Nuts,* and many other cookbooks. He has traveled extensively in North Africa and the Middle East, but lives in England, where he is the proprietor of three restaurants.